D1454201

WOMEN SPIES

By the same author:

DANGER FROM MOSCOW

FROGMAN EXTRAORDINARY

SCHOOL FOR SPIES

STALIN—THE MIRACULOUS GEORGIAN

THE TRAITOR TRADE

OUT OF THIS WORLD

HEALING HANDS

COMMANDER CRABB IS ALIVE

STRUGGLE IN THE DARK

THE FAKE DEFECTOR

HESS—THE MAN AND HIS MISSION

THE GREAT ILLUSION

ON THE OTHER SIDE OF REALITY

Co-authored:

THE PRIVATE LIFE OF JOSIF STALIN

THE PAIN AND THE GLORY

WOMEN SPIES

J. Bernard Hutton

W. H. ALLEN
LONDON & NEW YORK 1971

To

Harold, my son

© J. Bernard Hutton 1971

Photographs © U.P.I. London

Printed in Great Britain
for the publishers
W. H. Allen & Co. Ltd.,
Essex Street, London, WC2R 3JG
by The Anchor Press Ltd., Tiptree, Essex.
Bound in Tiptree by
Wm. Brendon & Son Ltd.

ISBN 0 491 00417 6

CONTENTS

Prologue

Day and night, year in and year out, Soviet and Western spies are as busy as beavers in every quarter of the globe. The daring, dangerous business of betraying nations never ceases. Hundreds of master spies masquerade under false names and personalities, and thousands of paid informers and agents feed them straws of information from which the bricks of military and political strategy are made.

Spying is a dangerous occupation and it is widely believed that women neither have the daring for this risky work nor the cool-nerved judgment it demands. When spy trials are headlines in the international Press it is always men who are depicted as the master spies, while the women involved are mere pawns; either wives who are loyal to their husbands, like Ethel Rosenberg in New York and Helen Kroger in London, or petty informers like Ethel Gee and Inge Block.

But Secret Service officers know better. There are many *ace* women spies. They are rarely trapped, therefore few of them receive headline publicity.

Is it that women are more skilful than men, and, like Greta Nielsson, brilliant at escaping detection?[1] Or does the subtle flavour of feminine charm in a man's world of danger give women an overwhelming advantage?

Fifty years after she died before a firing squad, Mata Hari's name is still a household word today. It brings to mind exotic love orgies between a beautiful, ruthless woman spy and military and political leaders. Mata Hari juggled history and brought

[1] Pages 68–76.

about bloody defeats and glorious victories alike to great armies. Spinning her web of charm around morally weak but powerful rulers, Mata Hari trifled with the destinies of great nations, outwitted Presidents and Prime Ministers, duped the monarchs and nobility of Europe and finally faced death courageously when she was unmasked as a spy.

This story is widely believed but completely untrue. It is a myth that persists in spite of documentary evidence that proves the 'Legend of Mata Hari' has almost no basis in fact.

Modern women spies are practical, hard-headed and hard-working. They'd laugh at the idea of lying in a Field Marshal's arms and coaxing his country's war secrets from him by seduction. They know well that sex is a woman spy's most deadly weapon; it must be used with a subtlety that would have been far beyond Mata Hari's ability to employ.

Margaretha Gertruida Zelle was a Dutch girl of eighteen when she answered a matrimonial advertisement that was to influence her future dramatically. She was irresistibly attractive to men but she secretly worried about her tendency to over-plumpness. She wanted an early marriage to secure a husband before she lost her figure as well as to sate her ardent sexual appetite.

The advertisement was inserted by a friend of a young Dutch officer named Macleod. The friend knew Macleod was home on leave from the East Indies and eager to meet charming young ladies. Macleod met Margaretha, was enchanted and proposed to her. She proved her generosity to him and as a result bore their child to the altar. Some time later the child was born in Indonesia.

The marriage was disastrous. Margaretha was lazy and a slut. She neglected her home, was soon bored with her husband and spent her days in a mad whirl of parties, dancing and love intrigues.

After the inevitable divorce, Margaretha returned alone to Europe. She had no desire to work for her living and devised a means by which she could employ her one undoubted talent without too much social stigma. She renamed herself Mata Hari, declared she was Indonesian by birth and advertised private 'exhibitions' of exotic, Indonesian dances.

No historian has ever provided evidence that Mata Hari's dancing was inspired, gifted or artistic. But her 'exhibition' was an instant success. The fame and notoriety of Mata Hari spread like wildfire, bringing her popularity and wealth. Her enthusiastic audiences were exclusively men and she often gave private performances for solitary male admirers.

The exotic flavour of Mata Hari's Indonesian dancing was enhanced by her nudity as she writhed her hips and her belly. But she never danced entirely naked. Her maiden fears of becoming over-plump were already justified and the passionate violence of her dancing demanded for her over-generous breasts the restraint of a jewelled brassière. Mata Hari would certainly not be regarded today as physically beautiful. But in her time she was a glamorous sex symbol who excited the imagination of men of all nationalities.

Cradled in luxury by many wealthy and influential lovers, Mata Hari lived with abandon, danced daringly throughout Europe and entertained countless admirers in her boudoir. Although she later vigorously denied all accusations of espionage, she boasted she'd been mistress to many influential men who had paid as much as £1,500 for a course of instruction in the intimate art of love-making.

Mata Hari's notoriety as a master spy began in 1917 when she was taken off a boat bound from Spain to Holland, and transported to France to stand trial. Reports of those court proceedings have been studied by experts and the consensus of legal opinion is that Mata Hari's trial was a travesty of justice that will forever shame France. Not one scrap of incriminating evidence can be found that would even justify Mata Hari's being brought to trial today.

Mata Hari came under suspicion because she travelled widely and had many influential lovers. This was not enough to bring such a serious charge as espionage against her. But then it was a time of national stress, the war was going badly for the Allies and the French were in a savage mood. If a woman even spoke sociably to the hated 'Boche', she aroused the blood lust of the mob. It was against this background of unreasoning hatred that Mata Hari was hustled through her trial to execution. Evidence to substantiate the charges against her was *never* produced in court; evidence that could have proved her innocence was suppressed.

Mata Hari was charged with spying against France. The prosecutor alleged that on the day war broke out she was seen in a car with Von Jagow, Chief of the Berlin police; therefore she was a spy. This absurd assertion showed the weakness of the State's case. Police chiefs are never involved in espionage, except to make arrests. Mata Hari's explanation that Von Jagow was one of her many lovers was undoubtedly true.

The prosecutor alleged Mata Hari became a German spy before the war with the Code Number H.21. In intercepted telegrams from a German master spy, she was referred to as H.21. Orders were given to make payments to her as Agent H.21.

Mata Hari admitted she was indeed H.21 and that she did receive payments through a German master spy. But the payment was for the intimate services she provided as his mistress and *not* for spying. Because the master spy could not afford to keep her from his own income, he placed her on his spy-roll. She was paid from official funds; as today an unscrupulous businessman might pay his mistress a salary through his firm and recoup on tax relief.

This doubtless genuine explanation given by Mata Hari was ridiculed and laughed out of court by the prosecutor and the judges. It was described as a 'fantastic' story and quite 'beyond belief'. Nevertheless, the history of espionage is studded with many similar examples and *it is now known that while Mata Hari was on trial, the Deuxième Bureau—the French Intelligence Service —was employing a woman spy who was receiving payment from the Germans under exactly the same circumstances.* Her name was Marthe Richer and she was one of the first woman aviators. Her husband was killed in the early days of the war. Burning for revenge against the Germans, she offered her services to the French Military Intelligence Force. Captain Ledoux knew how to use a beautiful woman spy and he sent Marthe Richer to Madrid with orders that she become the mistress of a German Naval

Attaché. During her long and intimate association with the German, Marthe sent back to France all the scraps of information she gleaned, which, when studied by military experts, were of invaluable aid to the Allies. But Marthe's German lover found the expense of his mistress too great a strain for his official pay packet. He too resorted to the ruse of placing his mistress on his spy list and paying for her extravagances from German Secret Service funds. Marthe informed Captain Ledoux of the Deuxième Bureau of this arrangement and, being an honest man, the captain wished to give evidence about this at Mata Hari's trial. He did not do so because he was *ordered* to remain silent.

It was also alleged that Mata Hari was at one time the mistress of a German Naval Attaché in Madrid. She did not deny this, since she had had so many lovers of various nationalities. But it was assumed—and charged—that she gave him secret information. Not a scrap of evidence was produced to prove she had done so, nor that she was ever in possession of such secret information.

The court was told that when Mata Hari realised she was under surveillance she attempted to avert suspicion of her loyalty by passing on secrets to French officials which she wormed out of a German lover. It was said Mata Hari warned that two German U-boats planned to land arms at the port of Mehadiya, for the use of Moroccan rebels who would harass the French Forces. Forewarned, French destroyers were said to have intercepted the German submarines and sunk them. The judges accepted these statements as true despite not one French official's having given verbal evidence of having received such information from Mata Hari. Years afterwards, when the fever of hatred bred by war had ebbed away, students of law discovered *there is no port in Morocco bearing the name Mehadiya and neither French nor German war records report German U-boats ever being sunk at any time off the Moroccan coast.*

Incredible as it now seems, accusation after accusation was flung at Mata Hari which her judges believed despite the lack of legal proof for the allegations being offered. A quick glance through her albums of press-cuttings, which were available to the court, would have instantly proved her innocent of many of the charges.

Even the most versatile woman spy cannot worm war secrets from over-sexed French officers in a French holiday resort at the same time as she is dancing before an enthralled male audience in Italy. It was alleged, again without any proof, that Mata Hari smuggled news to the Germans about the mutinies in the French Army during 1917. It was not until after the Armistice when censorship was relaxed that it was revealed that when the mutinies occurred, Mata Hari was already under arrest and awaiting trial. Subsequent inspection of German war records showed the Germans did not know about the French mutinies until long after they could have been turned to advantage by launching an all-out attack.

Thus, condemned by hearsay, rumour and prejudice Mata Hari was solemnly pronounced guilty of espionage and sentenced to death. At dawn on October 15th, 1917, still protesting her innocence, she was led out to the execution field, blindfolded and shot.

Why do we still talk about Mata Hari's notorious reputation as a spy when at her trial her accusers failed to prove one single act of espionage?

It is because of the face-saving strategy employed by the French Military High Command. The French Army had suffered shocking casualties; the bungling stupidity of its generals had sent loyal soldiers, like lambs, to the slaughter. War-weary men were senselessly flung into action again and again to gain a few yards of ground at enormous cost in blood. The tolerance of the men at the front reached breaking point and revolts broke out against the officers. The Military High Command abruptly faced up to the stark reality that the entire French Army might revolt.

The French High Command acted quickly to avert the disastrous consequences of its own incompetence. It proved to the Army that the Generals were *not* to blame for the appalling bloodshed at the front; it channelled the anger and resentment of its troops against the Germans and Mata Hari.

Mata Hari was the scapegoat for the French High Command. Her trial and execution were their vindication. When the Prosecutor pointed an accusing finger at Mata Hari and in a passionate, ringing voice, accused her of causing the deaths of more than fifty thousand loyal French soldiers and sailors, this charge was accepted by the judges. Yet no proof was provided that she caused the death of even one individual.

The entire French nation believed Mata Hari to be guilty long before she was brought into court. She entered the court already accused, tried and condemned. Her trial was a formality. The 'Big Lie' technique had been used skilfully; government departments had leaked so-called 'secret' information about her espionage activities. Officials sanctioned widespread rumours that her guilt was proved to the hilt, but added that State security would be embarrassed if that proof had to be made public. The rumours were embellished by imaginative minds, and incredible tales of Mata Hari's spying exploits were widely believed to be fact by a public hungry for sensation.

It is from this deliberate, semi-official fabrication of Mata Hari's espionage that her legend has sprung. Sir Basil Thomson, who was Chief of Scotland Yard's C.I.D., interrogated Mata Hari and later prepared a long report about her spying activities, which he honestly admitted was largely based on hearsay. But editors of sensational newspapers are reluctant to drop a meaty story about a beautiful woman spy, especially when she has a penchant for dancing in the nude. They accepted Sir Basil Thomson's long report as fact and enlarged upon it. They combed through it diligently, found facts which provided a hint to the validity of some of the wildest stories about Mata Hari's exploits, and fantasy became printed reality. Not until many years later was it realised that Sir Basil Thomson's report contained an obvious but vital error. He had dated all the incidents he reported *one year too early*! This mistake had encouraged sensation writers to link Mata Hari with spying activities which she could not possibly have been associated with. Even so, the 'Beautiful Spy Who Led Thousands To Death' story was too rich to be relinquished. Even after Mata Hari's execution the spying myth was expanded and embellished. The Kings, Princes and Prime Ministers who the legend claims to be her lovers made no dramatic last-minute attempt to save her life, for the simple reason that there was no truth in the rumours. The world learned of how the Marquis de Montessac had made a daring but unsuccessful rescue attempt. However, the sad truth is that no such person as the Marquis de Montessac ever existed, although in still another version of this fictional hero's valour, he was supposed to have bribed the execution squad to load their rifles with blank cartridges and bore away his loved one when she fell, apparently dead. Many romantically inclined people would like to believe Mata Hari thus escaped her fate and lived on in anonymity; but cold fact proves otherwise. It is Military Law that the officer in charge of a firing squad afterwards delivers the coup-de-grâce with a bullet from his own pistol.

The wilder the stories about Mata Hari, the longer they linger in the public's mind, especially one account of the way she met her death. A split second before the officer in charge of the execution squad gave the order to fire, Mata Hari threw open her fur coat to expose her completely naked body; whereupon every single man missed the target. Sober historical records, however, state that she did *not* go to her death in a fur coat and, even if she had, she could not have thrown it open with hands that were pinioned behind her and fastened to a post.

The Mata Hari legend was created by the French Military High Command, nourished by officially leaked (but invented) secret facts and blown up to mythical proportions by sensation writers. Despite many attempts to present the truth to the public, the legend still stirs people's imaginations and as a result any genuine woman spy in the news is promptly dubbed 'a second Mata Hari'.

The intelligent and skilful women spies described in this book are *genuine* spies, who do difficult and dangerous jobs efficiently. Unlike Mata Hari, they dare not bask in glamorous limelight, nor thrill to the admiration of captivated male admirers. But they do know that if their spying activities are detected, unlike Mata Hari, they will receive a scrupulously fair trial and the charges against them will have to be fully proved and substantiated with evidence.

1   Prelude to Espionage in the East

A basic rule of the Soviet Secret Service is to exercise far-sightedness in the selection of women spies and avoid recruitment of females 'who might prove to be the wrong types because mentally and physically they cannot withstand the difficult situations likely to confront them'.[1] They make unique precautions to ensure that only suitable candidates are chosen and no time is wasted in training anyone other than the most likely recruits. The following steps are taken to keep Moscow Secret Service Headquarters supplied with up-to-date lists of possible future agents:

Every Partorg[2] in each Communist Party cell throughout the U.S.S.R. has strict orders from the Orgleaders[3] of the Party's District Secretariats to 'secure full details about each comrade's private life, relatives, friends and acquaintances, their habits, hobbies, and any other details that throw light on their character and their life outside the Party'.[4] When all this information is checked and counter-checked, the Partorgs must submit detailed reports—which they must personally vouch for—to the Party District Secretariats' Orgleaders.

The Partorgs are trustworthy, hand-picked Party robots, but their reports are nevertheless again checked and sifted by the District Secretariats' Orgleaders. Exactly the same procedure is later followed by the Cadre Committee[5] of the Central Committee of the Communist Party of the U.S.S.R. A final short list,

[1] *Manual of the Soviet Secret Service Orgburo*, Moscow.
[2] Party Organiser.
[3] Organisation Leader.
[4] *Manual of the Soviet Secret Service Orgburo*, Moscow.
[5] The Department which decides whether an individual is to be considered reliable, unreliable, etc.

which is personally approved by the Head of the Cadre Committee, is then handed over to the Recruiting Division of the Moscow Secret Service Headquarters.

This first step in the selection of future Secret Service agents is still not finished. The Secret Service Recruiting Division at Moscow Headquarters is fully familiar with the painstaking precautions taken by the countless Partorgs, Orgleaders and the Cadre Committee, but they still do not accept the Party comrades' recommendations without further investigation. So the list of 'most reliable and suitable' men and women are passed on to the K.G.B.[1] to be reported upon by special investigators. These K.G.B. officers frequently lay traps for future Secret Service agents in order to 'check under extraordinary circumstances' his or her reliability and capability.

Women are the target for special investigation tests to ensure they are emotionally stable and suitable for a Secret Service career. Hard-hearted K.G.B. officers flirt with unsuspecting candidates, ply them with drink and seduce them. Only a Party-robot type who is unresponsive even when her attractive lover tries to make her say anything disloyal to the State is passed out as suitable for special service.

It is only when the final K.G.B. report reaches Moscow Secret Service Headquarters, and only if this report recommends the individual for a Secret Service career, that the candidate comes under consideration for possible recruitment.

The above procedure shows the care taken by Moscow Secret Service Headquarters to ensure that every Soviet spy is the best possible person for the job. Time, manpower and expense are no object. The Soviet Intelligence directors believe that time spent in the initial selection saves the waste of instructors' valuable time.

The prevailing opinion in most Intelligence Services of the Western world is that 'a good spy must be a born spy'. The Russian Secret Service believe that 'any person can be *taught* to be-

[1] *Komitet Gosudarstvennoye Bezopastnosti* = Committee (or Board) of State Security = Soviet Secret Police.

come an outstanding master spy, provided he or she is the right
raw-material for this highly skilled profession . . .'.[1]

When the spy candidates—who are quite unaware of the attention that has been devoted to them—are recommended to the
Secret Service Recruiting Division in Moscow, they are individually summoned to their Partorgs who will usually address them
as follows :

'. . . the Party in its far-sightedness and wisdom has selected
you for special schooling. You will appreciate this great honour
and will do everything in your power to become an outstanding
scholar, and not fail your Party that has such great hopes for
you . . .'.[2]

Whether this sudden and unsought 'honour' actually pleases
the chosen comrade, or not, is unimportant. When the Party decides to send a member on an assignment—whatever or wherever
it may be—no objections, not even on compassionate grounds,
are allowed. In many cases these orders come out of the blue, and
upset or even destroy family life. The disciplined Party member,
however, has no alternative but to obey and show enthusiasm.

It takes some time before the future agent is ordered to report
for duty; but when orders arrive they are only the first step on
the long road that leads to Secret Service schooling and training.

The starting point is always the Marx-Engels School, at Gorky,
near Moscow. This should not be confused with the Marx-Engels
Institute in Moscow, which is run by the Central Committee of
the Communist Party of the U.S.S.R. The former is the camouflaged primary school for future spies, run by the Recruiting
Division of the Moscow Secret Service Headquarters.

Throughout elementary training, students are kept under the
impression that they are being groomed for a Party career.

The Marx-Engels School at Gorky is one of a group of large
buildings which stand well back from the street and are surrounded

[1] *Manual of the Soviet Secret Service Orgburo,* Moscow.
[2] Example from 'how to inform recruits for special training', quoted from
Instructions to Partorgs, Moscow.

by high walls. All the entrances are guarded by State Security officers. Nobody is allowed in without a special pass.

On arrival at the Marx-Engels School, students are taken to the reception office where their passes are checked. Each student then surrenders his or her Party membership card, passport and all other identification documents and must then complete a long questionnaire.

The questionnaires are compared with those already completed and signed in the presence of the Partorgs many months previously. If there is the slightest discrepancy between the original and the present questionnaire—in most cases the only discrepancy is a question which is not answered in the same detail—the student is classed as 'unreliable'.

Students whose questionnaires show no discrepancy then undergo an entrance examination. This is a general-knowledge test aimed at ascertaining the education level and mental alertness of the individual. Few students fail, but in such cases the future spy is given a further test. Thus, students are admitted to the first stage of their Secret Service career.

Once the gate has closed behind him, all private life is at an end. For the duration of the elementary course, which usually lasts four months, the students at the Marx-Engels School are boarders who are forbidden to leave the school grounds without special permission. This is rarely granted. They are billeted in large dormitories on the buildings' upper floors; each dormitory accommodates twenty to forty students.

Their lives are organised collectively and their minds are conditioned by those in charge of the establishment.

Every student signs a statement that at no time will he or she communicate to anybody, in any way, anything about the school. They also undertake 'to work to the best of my ability and to spare no effort nor energy to become an outstanding specialist in the fields to which I may be transferred'.

For these first four months the students devote themselves exclusively to the study of the *History of the World Workers' Movement*, and the *History of the Communist Party of the U.S.S.R.*

Their daily routine is as follows:

07.00 hours: Get up.
07.25 hours: Assembly at the physical training ground.
07.30 hours: Physical training.
08.00 hours: Breakfast.
08.30 hours: Assemble in classroom and preparation for lecture.
09.15 hours: Lecture.
10.45 hours: Break.
11.00 hours: Lecture.
12.30 hours: Lunch.
13.00 hours: Assembly in the Meeting Hall. Reading of daily newspapers.
13.45 hours: Assembly in classroom and preparation for the next lecture.
14.00 hours: Lecture.
15.30 hours: Break. To be used for the preparation for the next lecture.
15.45 hours: Lecture.
17.15 hours: Assembly in the Meeting Hall. Lecture on daily events and discussion.
18.25 hours: Assembly at physical training ground.
18.30 hours: Physical training.
19.15 hours: Supper.
20.00 hours: Assembly in classroom, homework.
21.00 hours: Assembly in the Meeting Hall, films or television.
22.30 hours: Bed.

This strict régime, which regulates every student's life from morning till night, is regarded even by fanatically loyal Party members as 'over-organisation'.

It has been devised for the following purposes:

1. To constantly remind students that they are attending a special Party school.

2. To ensure that every student is thoroughly schooled in Communist ideology and accustomed to thinking and acting like a classic Bolshevik.

The students are not told that they are under consideration as possible Secret Service agents. Nor do they know they are under constant observation to test their suitability for this specialised profession.

2 Practical Training

When the first stage of preliminary schooling is completed, those in charge of the Marx-Engels School are able to gauge the future work for which each student is suited. But the rules of the Secret Service require final gradings to be made only when it is established for which practical tasks each student is best suited. So, after four months, the second stage of the preliminary schooling begins. The students are transferred to the Lenin Technical School, Verkhovnoye—some ninety miles from Kazan.

This school is situated in a desolate area near the border of the Tatar Autonomous Soviet Republic and is only accessible by a private road. It is virtually inaccessible to anyone not connected with it. The huge complex building sprawls over several square miles and is fenced in by a high brick wall. All entrances are closely guarded on the inside by armed State Security officers.

When the students from the Marx-Engels School in Gorky arrive at Verkhovnoye they are taken once again to the reception office. This time they are *not* required to pass a stringent security check. They have been transported by K.G.B. vehicles direct to their destination. No outsider could possibly 'infiltrate en route'.

The school is a modern building and the students are again billeted in large dormitories on the upper floors. The working schedule in this institution is as 'over-organised' as in the previous one. No politics are taught and the students concentrate on practical training for the following twelve months. There is a student centre where students can dance to the radio or record-players, or see films. But their strict time-table leaves them little time for recreation.

Surprisingly, despite this militaristic discipline, the students are content. They study interesting and useful subjects and rarely suspect they are attending a Secret Service school. They respect the secrecy ruling and do not attempt to tell their relatives or friends the name or whereabouts of the Lenin Technical School in Verkhovnoye. They correspond, but through a supplied accommodation address. All Russian Party members are well-disciplined and accept the ruling that 'strictest precautions must be taken to prevent enemies of the State from obtaining important information'.

The twelve months' course at the Lenin Technical School in Verkhovnoye starts with a month of physical training.

The Russians believe that only students in excellent physical condition can be fully mentally alert. Great importance is placed upon intensive physical training. If students at a later date are found unsuitable for Secret Service work, the hard training they have received will have 'steeled' them for other useful work.

The physical training is similar to the commando-training practised in other countries. Both male and female students undergo arduous courses, climbing steep hills, walls and difficult obstacles, jumping from heights, crossing muddy marshes, rivers and tough terrains while fully clothed, climbing roof-tops, scaling treacherous mountain paths and walking for long distances over rock-strewn ground while carrying heavy equipment.

This physical training always produces a crop of minor and major casualties. But both male and female students believe that 'steeling' their bodies is of paramount importance to them, and their country.

The physical training course is followed by self-defence tuition —jiu-jitsu, judo, karate and other forms of attack and defence. It includes unconventional boxing and wrestling styles to ensure students can take care of themselves in any difficult situation.

Self-defence, boxing, wrestling and jiu-jitsu are taught in all Russian elementary and secondary schools as well as in factories and offices, so this course is an extension of the students' previous training. They undergo an intensive two weeks' course of training for six hours daily.

The next stage of training is handling firearms. Both male and female students are trained to shoot with revolvers, pistols, rifles and sub-machine guns. This course lasts only one week but every student must pass out with top marks. They rarely fail because all Party members and other trusted Soviet citizens are used to handling firearms of all kinds at their places of work or study.

In addition to marksmanship, the students are taught to handle explosives of all kinds. The five weeks' 'explosives' course teaches students how to destroy bridges, buildings and other important or strategic targets. Dynamite, T.N.T., gelignite and plastic explosives are used and students are taught to make home-made bombs. All this training takes place on the 'Explosive Training Ground' situated in the northern part of the school's grounds, at a safe distance from the main buildings. Specially built iron and concrete practice targets are provided for the planting of time-bombs and for detonating them effectively from a safe distance. Students also learn how to look for concealed time-bombs and booby-traps and render them harmless.

One section of this phase of training concentrates on blowing locks, strong-room doors and 'burglar-proof' safes. Students are taught to assess the type of explosive most suitable for any particular job and how to muffle explosions.

Finally, students learn how to conceal small but powerful explosives in cigarette boxes, lighters, pens, match-boxes and other articles which are in everyday use.

The students of the Lenin Technical School are now ready for specific tuition and practical training in operations which they may have to carry out when working in foreign lands as agents of the Soviet Secret Service. But there is an 'in between' course of instruction on how to prepare doped or poisoned drinks, chocolates and food, cigarettes and cigars. Students learn which drugs are most effective for a specific task, how long it takes before the drugs become effective, and what are the victim's symptoms. Doping and poisoning is considered an important part of a Soviet agent's training. Students are also taught to tap telephone lines and how to utilise high-power 'limpet' microphones.

A month is also spent showing students how to record tapped telephone and other conversations, and how to 'doctor' recordings. At the end of their training cadet spies can 'doctor' recordings so efficiently that the original recorded speech is completely changed in its meaning and not even experts can detect it as a forgery. Agents operating abroad use these recordings to blackmail selected victims and force them to become informers. If a 'doctored' recording cannot be used for 'recruiting' an informer it can often be used for propaganda purposes. The Soviet Secret Service also makes extensive use of 'limpet' microphones and spy wire recorders which are standard equipment for agents working in enemy territory.

Each subject taught at the Lenin Technical School is considered of vital importance, and every student is expected to score full marks at all intermediary examinations. But operating portable short-wave radio receiver-transmitters and taking photographs are classified as the most important subjects of the course. Students not only practise how 'to receive and pass on radio messages under difficult conditions', they also learn to use special appliances which enable them to broadcast at lightning speed, a method that cuts down transmission to mere seconds, and which deprives foreign counter-intelligence of any chance of locating the transmitter. They also practise coding and decoding, and learn 'taking every possible precaution to prevent planted messages from foreign Intelligence agents being accepted as a message from headquarters'. They learn by heart all call signs and instruction signals. They are trained to service breakdowns of small but effective long-range radio receiver-transmitters, dismantle and reassemble them and are expected to locate any defect within minutes.

The last phase of this twelve months' course is devoted to practical photography; developing and touching-up pictures without the trickery being detected. The cadets must be expert at making copies of blueprints, technical drawings and maps. They also learn to transform microfilms into microdots which can be concealed under postage stamps. They handle all types of microfilm cameras so that they will not be handicapped if their own is damaged.

According to the school records at Verkhovnoye, every student of the full twelve months' course *always* passes the final examinations. This is not surprising. During the course intermediate tests weed out students who are below standard. Those who fail intermediary exams are given intensive training, work longer hours and soon catch up with the others.

The final examinations occupy an entire working week. But even top marks do not provide automatic entrance into the Soviet Secret Service. The Board of the Lenin Technical School has no say about this—it can only indicate the future potential of each student. It is the Secret Service Selection Board that considers the final examination results and the weekly progress reports compiled by instructors about each student to reach a decision. And while the Selection Committee ponders upon its decisions, the students are sent for a month's holiday to the Oktyabr Recreation Centre in the Caucasian mountain spa of Kyslovodsk.

A student who has passed the final examinations at the Marx-Engels School, Gorky, and at the Lenin Technical School, Verkhovnoye, is seldom found unsuitable for 'special activities'. Those few who are rejected are told at the end of their holiday that they are to return to their former jobs to await a new assignment. Most of them are later elevated to the status of Partorg without ever knowing they were novice spy candidates.

Those graded 'suitable for foreign service' are assigned to 'assessment duties' at Moscow Secret Service Headquarters, while those classified 'suitable for home duties' go to Moscow K.G.B. Headquarters.

The figures for 1970[1] disclose that of the 3,072 students who passed the final examinations at the Lenin Technical School, Verkhovnoye, 2,094 were sent for 'assessment duties' in Moscow Secret Service Headquarters. The remaining 978 went to the K.G.B.

'Assessment duties' at Moscow Secret Service Headquarters usually last from ten to twelve months. Cadets are split up into working groups which enables the Selection Board of the Recruiting Division at Moscow Headquarters to concentrate its attention on one group of cadets at a time to assess the most suitable work for each candidate, and the country to which he or she should be sent.

Cadets study the routine duties of specialised officers in their specific division, and give close attention to the comprehensive reports on the day-to-day work of Soviet agents in the field. 'Assessment duties' at Moscow Headquarters are the most exhausting part of a cadet's training.

This is what one candidate wrote :

'. . . I realised at the beginning that if I wanted to comprehend and visualise the many varieties of the extensive special tasks and situations which I daily came across during my twelve months at the Foreign Directorate, I had to take task-work back to the hostel every evening. I spent almost all my free evenings studying. I am happy that I followed the example of my other comrades and decided to do homework. This was the only thing that enabled me to pass all my interim tests and be recommended for further schooling . . .'[2]

An editorial note in the next issue of this same publication took the candidate's contribution further by adding that the other students on 'assessment duties' all wished it to be known that the candidate's article also applied to them.

Feliks Edmundovich Dzhierzhinsky, the founder of the Soviet

---

[1] *Manual of the Soviet Secret Service Orgburo,* Moscow.
[2] Quoted from *M.V.D. Information,* Moscow.

Secret Service, once said : 'The real *Chekist* is steeled and stable; nothing can shake him !'

This still holds good. Today's hand-picked members of the Soviet Intelligence network are such devoted Bolsheviks that they will blindly carry out any assignment, and will always remain loyal to those who elevated them to the 'élite' of the Soviet Union.

3   Mock Arrests

After two and a half years' preliminary training, Moscow's Secret Service directors are satisfied that all the cadets on their short list of future agents are absolutely devoted to the cause of Soviet Russia. Nevertheless, they test how each stands up to 'treatment'. They assume that foreign counter-espionage interrogators habitually use brainwashing, third degree and other modern methods of extracting information and confessions from the spies they arrest. The Soviet spy tutors try to break down their own pupils under simulated interrogation pressures.

Shortly before the Selection Board of the Recruiting Division at Moscow Headquarters makes its final decision, mock arrests are made. None of those arrested know they are being subjected to yet another test. They believe it is a genuine arrest.

The procedure follows a standard pattern.

The Secret Service candidate is individually 'arrested'. She does not know if anyone shares her fate. She is given no reason for her arrest and is transported to State Security Headquarters. There she is taken to the Investigation Block and ordered to stand motionless, facing a wall. She is ordered to clasp her hands behind her neck. This is mild first-degree treatment. The victim finds it increasingly difficult to keep her balance and remain completely still.

Only those who have been forced to stand like this for hours, facing a wall, can know what a severe strain it can be. I suffered this treatment in Russia. My hands, arms, feet and head became heavier every minute and I ached in every part of my body, even to the joints of my fingers. Leaden weariness weighed down my limbs. I broke out in a cold sweat and my body itched unbearably. I felt impelled to scratch but the guard saw my movement and clubbed me warningly with his rifle butt. Time and again I thought I could endure the strain no longer. Yet I did. And the long hours dragged slowly by.

When the interrogator decides enough 'mild treatment' has been applied the arrested student is brought to his office. There she is accused of being a foreign spy who has wormed into the Soviet Secret Service. The accused is naturally astonished, unable to understand how such an accusation can be made, and denies everything. Usually she tries to explain a mistake must have been made, but the interrogator shouts, threatens and demands a confession.

When the accused stubbornly refuses to make a confession, she is locked up in a cell. But as soon as the exhausted prisoner sits on her bunk or falls asleep, a guard rushes in and herds the prisoner back to the interrogator.

This time the victim is placed in front of a blinding arc-light. The interrogator says he no longer cares if the accused confesses because he is now in possession of a confession signed by the accused's accomplice. He says he has sufficient evidence to justify the accused being shot, even without her confession.

All victims of mock arrests are dazed and bewildered. They are devoted Bolsheviks and cannot understand how anyone can believe such accusations against them. They try to explain this. But the interrogator again thumps the desk, shouts and threatens.

This type of interrogation goes on for at least twenty-four hours. The interrogators are changed every few hours but the prisoner is re-interrogated as soon as she yields to exhaustion and falls asleep in the cell.

Some interrogators use physical violence to break the victim's resistance. Women as well as men are subjected to severe man-handling. The Secret Service Manual warns: '. . . The practice of causing *extreme* bodily harm to candidates who undergo extensive resistance tests must cease. It is forbidden that future operators be injured while establishing if they are mentally and physically strong enough to resist great pressure . . .'. But the manual adds: 'Moderate measures of physical violence may be utilised to ascertain if future agents are likely to yield to torture at the hands of foreign interrogators.'

Before 'arrested' cadets are subjected to mock brainwashing, they are threatened to be 'shot forthwith without trial' unless they sign a prepared confession. Having endured all the previous tests, the candidate usually refuses. An armed State Security officer then escorts the prisoner back to the cell.

The prisoner is now subjected to brainwashing which is carried out by experts. It is not necessary to describe this stage in detail, for Soviet Russia's methods of brainwashing are already well known. According to Moscow statistics, 'since 1957, no cadet Secret Service agent lost control of his or her own will while being brainwashed'. But when at last this strenuous interrogation phase is completed, and the interrogators are satisfied the candidate is 'break proof', the arrested cadet is led to an assembly room where she is addressed by one of the heads of the Soviet Secret Service. The reasons for the interrogation is explained and, strange as it may seem, none of the victims resent having been physically manhandled and brainwashed. Perhaps they are too relieved to learn the nightmare experience has been just another test.

Before being 'set free', each cadet is pledged to keep this 'loyalty test' a sacred secret from other cadets. Those to undergo this test in the future must be taken quite unawares. The 'proved' cadet signs an oath of secrecy.

Ability and reliability tests are now at an end. The final grading and assessment for future service is made and the chosen men and women are enrolled as officers of the Soviet Secret Service. They are now ready for long-range schooling which often endures ten years before they begin work in the field as a master spy.

4 Russia's Remarkable Spy Schools

The most unique of the Soviet's schools for spies is a specialised establishment known as Gaczyna. It lies a hundred miles south-east of Kuibyshev. The school grounds, covering an area of some forty-two square miles, stretch along the south of the Tatar Autonomous Soviet Republic to the Bashkir Autonomous Soviet Republic.

Without a Secret Service permit no one can get near Gaczyna. The entire zone is guarded by crack State Security detachments who seal off the whole terrain for a radius of thirty miles.

Soviet Intelligence directors take every precaution to keep this top-secret establishment under wraps. It does not appear on any map and to the Russian people's knowledge, and that of the world, it does not exist. By this time, the students have been told the truth about their future work as Soviet spies and when they are flown by special M.V.D.[1] aircraft to Gaczyna they find themselves in completely foreign surroundings.

Gaczyna is the school in which future Soviet Secret agents for the English-speaking world are trained. To give cadets a thorough habilitation background to the English-speaking world, Gaczyna is divided up as follows :

In the north-west :	North-American section.
In the north :	Canadian section.
In the north-east :	United Kingdom section.
In the south :	Australian, New Zealand, Indian and South African sections.

Each division is a completely independent zone and quite se-

[1] *Ministerstvo Vnutrennykh Dyel*—Interior Ministry.

parate from any of the other 'countries'. Moscow Secret Service
Headquarters wants each cadet, from the start of her super schooling at Gaczyna, to live in the environment of the country which
she will eventually adopt.

Although most newcomers to Gaczyna know only the English
they have learned at school, they are ordered henceforth to speak
only the language of their chosen country, even if they can barely
make themselves understood. They are ordered to forget their
Russian nationality and assume a completely new identity. Russia's Secret Service directors believe that it takes ten years for a
human brain to become conditioned to a new personality. And
after this, any agent caught by foreign counter-intelligence will
stick to his adopted identity as though it were truly his own. Not
even torture, brainwashing or truth drugs will make him con-
fess otherwise.

Gaczyna schooling has been proved immensely successful.
Soviet spies in all parts of the English-speaking world easily pass
themselves off as nationals of the countries which they claim to
come from. The notorious Gordon Lonsdale is a good example.
When caught and questioned, and throughout his trial at the
Old Bailey, he fervently insisted he was Gordon Lonsdale, despite
Scotland Yard's Special Branch having established he was Russian. The cases of Rita Elliott,[1] Eileen[2] and others are equally
striking examples of Gaczyna-trained master spies who successfully concealed their Russian identities.

On arrival at Gaczyna cadets are taken straight to the 'country' to which the Selection Board of the Recruiting Division in
Moscow has assigned them. For the next ten years they never
leave this zone.

Every division of Gaczyna is an accurate replica of typical
streets, buildings, cinemas, restaurants, snack bars, public houses
and other typical establishments in countries of the English-
speaking world. Everyone wears the clothes of these countries.
The inhabitants occupy rooms in boarding houses or hotels, apart-

[1] Chapter 7.
[2] Chapter 8.

ments or houses which are identical to those in America, England and elsewhere. From the first day of their arrival the student spies are plunged into typical Western surroundings.

To duplicate the conventions of life in the chosen countries, the male and female inhabitants of Gaczyna occupy the same hotels, apartments and houses, and are no longer expected to avoid developing personal friendships. But, even when alone together, cadets have strict orders to speak only English. If an instructor or senior student overhears 'first formers' speaking Russian, they are reported for disobedience. The culprits are fined and a repetition of the offence ends their spy career.

The first five years for every newcomer to Gaczyna means a concentrated study of the English language. They are not only taught grammar, the right construction of sentences and special idioms, but special attention is paid to pronunciation. The students listen to tape-recorded B.B.C., N.B.C., C.B.S. and other broadcasts, and perfect their knowledge of the language until they are able to pass out as sons or daughters of the country which they are supposed to come from.

All the language masters at Gaczyna are hand-picked Communist Party members who have come from America, England and other countries of the English-speaking world. They are trusted teachers who have become Soviet citizens and have broken all ties with their former countries.

They are by no means the only foreigners employed at Gaczyna. To enable the students to live in typical Western surroundings, the waitresses, shop assistants, bus conductors and workers in all other professions are also ex-citizens of the designated country, who have become Soviet citizens and qualified for these special jobs. They are all life-timers in Gaczyna because the Soviet Secret Service will not release them and risk their talking outside. Even though they are devoted Communist Party members, the Russians never completely trust their foreign comrades.

Among the fully trusted Western citizens who left their countries of birth to become loyal Russian Party robots are Melinda Maclean (ex-Cominform instructor and wife of the runaway British Foreign Office official Donald Maclean), and Bernon

B

Mitchel, an American cipher clerk; scores of other Communists from the West, whose names did not make headlines in the international Press, have also slipped quietly behind the Iron Curtain to serve Soviet Russia in Gaczyna.

Thus, every cadet rubs shoulders with genuine ex-citizens of their 'adopted' country, and hears the correct language pronunciation and intonation. Not only language teachers but everyone is under orders to correct any student, at any time, who makes a grammatical mistake or mispronounces a word.

The first months at Gaczyna are a strain for students. Despite their determination to master their new language they make slow headway. They spend long hours developing their vocabulary, learning sentence construction and repeating pronunciations endlessly played to them on gramophone records. They have long conversations with waitresses, shop assistants and other English-born people whom they meet every day, and they spend a great deal of time in the cinema watching American and English films brought in from the West. They get the feel of life in the West, as well as familiarising themselves with its language and background.

The effectiveness of the tuition in Gaczyna is best shown by an account published by the Ministry of the Interior Journal. It is signed with the initials 'F.K.'. A Secret Service student writes:

'It is really amazing how quickly one can learn a foreign language if one is really determined to work hard . . .

When I arrived at the school, I knew hardly any English. It was the same with most of the others. The strict rule of prohibiting the speaking of Russian from the moment of arrival at the school is really the only effective way of forcing one's brain to think in the foreign language. One makes headway considerably more quickly than if this practice had not been a definite *must*.

. . . At the beginning it was very hard, and almost all of us could hardly speak to each other. But soon this changed. First in basic English, then at a higher level, we soon learned to converse with each other.

. . . I am amazed how much of a language one can learn in a little more than six months. This is mainly due to the many excellent forms of tuition and also to the fact that we all are determined to master the language as soon as possible . . .

Thanks to this system of tuition, and to our teachers, we are all now able to talk freely with each other, to read and write and to understand most of what is said in English broadcasts and films. Also, our Masters tell us that our pronunciation is improving from day to day. . . .'[1]

F.K.'s account is not an exaggeration. Statistics at Gaczyna and at Moscow Secret Service Headquarters confirm this report. Even more striking confirmation of the excellence of the schooling are the many Soviet spies themselves—in America, England, Australia, New Zealand, Canada, South Africa, Northern Ireland and Eire, India and other parts of the English-speaking world— all of whom were schooled at Gaczyna and who have successfully managed to pass as citizens of the countries they claim to come from.

The Gaczyna spy school is divided into sectors for America, Canada, the United Kingdom, Australia, New Zealand, India and South Africa. Teaching in each zone follows the same pattern, the only difference being that each individual zone duplicates the environment of the designated country, and that the teachers and other staff are ex-natives of the specified country.

The zone for the United Kingdom, which stretches over some sixty square miles, is divided into a city and a rural area. The future resident operators become fully familiar with what would have been their background if they had grown up in the United Kingdom.

The city area is a true replica of a typical London suburb. It has a High Street, many shops, cafés, public houses, restaurants, banks, a post office and a cinema. The shops are stocked with goods manufactured in England. Apart from all articles of English clothing, foodstuffs, cigarettes, confectionery and other com-

[1] Quoted from *M.V.D. Information,* Moscow.

modities, the inhabitants buy English newspapers and magazines and acquaint themselves with British journalism and conventions as will any British-born person. All inhabitants of the United Kingdom zone receive a weekly salary of £40, paid in English currency. Out of this they pay their rent and buy food, clothing and the other necessities of life at prices currently ruling in England. The Soviet Embassy in London regularly supplies Moscow with current prices, enabling Gaczyna to make price adjustments. Cadets are as fully aware of everyday conditions and changing values in Britain as any complaining British housewife.

The Russian students, who not so long ago lived in typical Soviet surroundings in Moscow, Leningrad, Kiev, Minsk or Baku, quickly grow acclimatised to their way of life.

After a while, they no longer stare in wonder at red double-decker London buses, nor laugh at the unfamiliar sight of red letter-boxes on the kerbside. They queue at the cinema box-offices, enjoy smoking English-brand cigarettes, eat fish and chips, complain about English licensing hours and acquire a taste for beer which, at first, they usually dislike. With every passing day they become more 'English'.

The rural area comprises a small village and a section of a country town. Both are duplicates that could have been a transplant from an English county. No red London buses, only Green Line and Corporation vehicles, roar along these roads.

The 'rural' inhabitants of Gaczyna enjoy country inns, the weekly dances in the Social Hall and the way of life of the English countryside. To familiarise cadets with life in cities, towns and villages, the students spend a third of their ten years' stay at Gaczyna in a London suburb, a third in a rural town and a third in a village.

The inhabitants of Gaczyna live an Englishman's routine day. They start it with a breakfast of cereal, eggs and bacon; or fish, tea, toast and marmalade. They then take a bus to school. At lunch they go to the 'local' where, with half a pint of beer, they have a snack; or they go to a Wimpy Bar, a café, a restaurant or an Espresso. They dine at their own home or that of a friend. But regardless of whether it is homemade or restaurant food, it is always an English meal, cooked, served and eaten in English style.

Although most cadets believe that after a year's stay in Gaczyna they really know *all* about their 'country of birth', they nevertheless frequently meet something new. An example of this is illustrated by the following extract from a letter a student sent to a Section Leader in the Second Division of the Foreign Directorate at Moscow Secret Service Headquarters:

'I suddenly developed a terrible toothache and had to see a dentist. How different this dental surgery was from any other I've seen anywhere in the U.S.S.R.

First I was seen by a receptionist in a smart white coat. After she had spoken to the dentist over the intercom, she led me to a comfortably furnished waiting room which had plenty of journals on the table. . . .

After a short wait the dentist came and led me to his surgery. This too was completely different from anything we know. There were not eight or more dentists' chairs in a row with dentists attending patients; there was only one chair, and the dentist had his own assistant.

The dentist told me that he had to extract my tooth and asked whether I liked gas. When I told him I wasn't fussy and that I was used to having a tooth pulled out without anaesthetics, he told me he would extract my tooth as he always does. In no time I was under the anaesthetic. . . .'

After years at Gaczyna, the future Soviet master spy destined for the Western world really knows the Western way of life.

5 Learning the 'English' Way

Gaczyna's function is to educate future operators in all fields of espionage in America, England and other English-speaking countries. For the first five years cadets undergo the 'Anglo-Saxon acclimatisation period'.

During the first year almost three-quarters of all study time is devoted to English language tuition, but lesson time is reduced each year until in the fifth year it takes up only half of all study hours. By then the student has complete command of the language and can pass as a citizen of any chosen Western country. Yet schooling continues for another five years. Gaczyna takes no chances.

Gaczyna's pupils are educated on the same lines as schoolchildren and university students in America, the United Kingdom, Australia, etc. They attend history and general knowledge classes, they read classics and modern authors and are even required to listen to gramophone records of traditional and popular Western music, folk-songs and pop music. They are taught ballroom and other styles of dancing.

There is a regular screening of educational films, and lectures illustrated with photographs and colour slides. Students later write detailed essays on the subject and discuss it in their classrooms with their lecturers.

Every inhabitant of Gaczyna must attend the 'exhibition halls for special education'. These are wardrobe museums. One of them, commonly referred to by the students of Gaczyna as the 'Junkshop', contains dummies dressed in all uniforms in current use.[1]

---

[1] The exhibition described here is in the United Kingdom division. Every other division in Gaczyna has similar exhibition halls each with a collection of uniforms, etc., of the particular country concerned.

The future Secret Service operators are expected to memorise these uniforms thoroughly. On the ground floor, in the Military Department, is shown every type of Army, Royal Navy, and Royal Air Force uniform—including the Guards and other special regiments. There is also a comprehensive collection of badges, and students learn to recognise every Service rank; they must know by heart all decorations, medals and badges, and are subjected to many snap examination tests about them.

On the second floor are the uniforms of constables and officers of the Metropolitan Police, the City of London Police and the police forces of every county in the United Kingdom. On the third floor are uniforms of firemen, postmen and railwaymen, special guards and other similar everyday uniforms. No cadet is ever likely to mistake one uniform for another. In international espionage, fatal unmaskings are likely to occur because of such 'stupid slips'.

Other 'exhibition halls for special education' display railway coaches, buffet and Pullman cars. Still another exhibition hall consists of well-known London landmarks including illuminated replicas of Piccadilly Circus, the Houses of Parliament, Westminster Abbey and the Bank of England. They even display models of the interiors of department stores, and other places considered important enough for students to memorise.

Combined with films and lectures, maps and guide books, this method of tuition makes the future spies thoroughly at home in their new 'countries of birth' before ever setting foot in them.

Although students at Gaczyna are good at sport as a result of their training in elementary and secondary schools, and later at the Lenin Technical School, Verkhovnoye, they nevertheless find it difficult to understand Anglo-Saxon sport which is vastly different from their own. Cricket is their greatest headache. They find it difficult to grasp the rules and technique of cricket. They are shown films on cricket, but despite continuous practice. it takes them a long time to feel they have mastered the sport. Russians play baseball, basket-ball, football and most other world sports, but they find it hard to adapt themselves to the American and English rules of the game.

When a master spy is finally sent abroad as a Resident Network Operator, he or she is often required to become a 'respectable business personality'. It is therefore essential for him to know as much as possible about business methods.

The future 'business people' take courses in shorthand, are trained on Western typewriters and receive tuition in book-keeping and general office routine. Those who were technical experts before being selected for Secret Service work undergo courses to familiarise them with English technical terms. All students are taught banking, exporting and importing procedure, how to make income tax returns and the other routine subjects a business executive would know. They study the Stock Exchange and are expected to know the names of the most important public companies.

There is even a course of instruction on Common Law; the Western world's civil law and criminal law is vastly different from the judiciary system of the Soviet Union. Cadets must also know the Highway Code and learn to drive different types of American and English cars.

And throughout this long training the students speak in English, think in English and live in English.

The second five years' term at Gaczyna trains future master spies for the English-speaking world in coding, decoding and call-sign techniques. This is a refresher course since the students have already received a thorough technical training during their year's stay at the Lenin Technical School in Verkhovnoye. But its scope is much more extensive. Moscow believes that 'a thousand precautions are better than one mistake', and insists upon the memorising of a system of seven codes used in irregular rotation. Students must master seven completely different codes and call-sign systems.

Moscow is confident these codes and secret call-sign techniques cannot be broken by even the best Western code experts. Nevertheless, Soviet Secret Service Headquarters insure against 'code-cracking' by employing this 'seven section' code and call-sign system.

This is how it works:

Each code has its identification name: Martyn, Oslo, Steve, Kiel, Venus, Alma, North. The Resident Network Operator in a foreign country is told which of the seven codes and call-sign systems he is to use for the first incoming or outgoing message. If he uses Alma for number one message, then at the end of the message he states which of the other codes will be used next time. If the chosen code for the following message is Martyn, then Moscow will transmit the next message in the Martyn code. Resident Operators use the different codes in irregular sequence.

Each of the seven codes and call-sign systems is fundamentally different. One code key would be useless for decoding another. And to exclude the possibility of any counter-intelligence service breaking the codes, Moscow frequently changes the entire code system.

It is impossible for anyone, other than a Resident Network Operator of the present-day Soviet Secret Service or a senior Soviet espionage agent, to give away these seven codes and call-sign systems because of these frequent changes. It is possible, however, to expose one code which is constantly used.[1] It is the oldest but the most efficient. It is known as 'Kiel' and works as follows:

A particular book is chosen as the key for the code, and the page to be used for the start of each message is stated. If, for instance, it is page eleven then the coding or de-coding of the message starts on the first line of page eleven.

The next step—both for coding and decoding—is to find the required letter of the message in the first line of the book page. Every single letter, space, comma, colon, semi-colon, full stop, etc., is counted, and the number of the letter is written down in the coded message. If the required letter is not found in the line a 'o' is written down. This sometimes applies to several successive lines on a key book page, for the strict rule is that only one letter in every line on the key book page is used.

[1] This code is successfully and continuously used by the Soviet Government and the World Communist Movement.

When deciphering the message, the coding clerk or Resident Network Operator know when seeing a 'o' that they must go on to the next line on the key book page. They then count the letters in the line until they come to the required letter.

The Kiel code is very simple and clear because spaces between words, commas, full stops, etc., are clearly shown in the messages; but anyone who does not know the code key, and the page of the key book on which the message starts, is unable to decode the message because there is no repetition of letters.

If at any time a change of the key book is decided upon, such a change is transmitted in a coded message.

The other six code and call-sign systems work on entirely different lines. Most use letters and number combinations. But because the systems are changed so frequently, and *always* when a Resident Network Operator is arrested by Western counter-intelligence services, the composition of the remaining six code systems is not known.

When Gaczyna's pupils have mastered the code and call-sign system, they switch to radio communications. This is a continuation of what they have already learned and practised at Verkhovnoye. They spend little time on dismantling and reassembling radio receiver-transmitters and instead concentrate upon the technique of transmitting and receiving messages with modern, high-speed methods. They use equipment that can transmit messages in seconds, which would otherwise require several minutes. They are introduced to a scientific 'aid' which distorts their voices to strangers, yet is understandable to those for whom the messages are intended. Every precaution is being taken so that no Russian spy is ever likely to be confronted by an intercepted recording of his or her voice in the event of arrest.

Radio communication is considered good only for supplementary transmissions. Moscow fears that the too-frequent use of radio receiver-transmitters enables Western counter-intelligence to locate the operators, even if they use portable sets in cars travelling through remote country lanes.

A method of communication which the Soviet Secret Service favours most is the use of microdots. Equipped with the finest apparatus, both the Resident Network Operators abroad and Moscow Secret Service Headquarters can reduce long documents or messages to pin-head size. Detailed messages, running into many pages, can be recorded on several microdots, and the complete message passed on in one transmission. The laboratories at Gaczyna specialise in microdots and are better equipped than those at the Lenin Technical School, so the students learn about every microdot innovation.

The customary method of receiving and sending microdot messages is under postage stamps of ordinary business or private letters. The microdots are protected from damage by the glue of the stamp, and the letters are not sent direct to Iron Curtain countries but reach their destination by a roundabout route—being received and passed on by apparently innocent 'in-between stations'. This method is slow but Moscow prefers the 'safe' way.

Training in microdot technique at Gaczyna covers taking and despatching microfilms of blueprints and confidential documents. At Gaczyna the 'passing on' of such information is a study in itself. Most of the 'safe' ways are known to Western counter-intelligence, but many of the Russians' ingenious methods, which could have been invented by a thriller writer, are not commonly known about.

Considerable time is spent by students in practising how to convert commonly used, everyday articles into microfilm containers.

A travel alarm clock, for instance, is a good hiding place. Without interfering with the mechanism of the clock, spies can conceal a microfilm inside it, containing top-secret blueprints, scientific calculations or documents. The clock works normally and when a carrier goes abroad on a business trip, there is no reason why Customs or Security Officers should suspect a merrily ticking clock.

Another favourite hiding place for microfilm is inside an electric toothbrush. There is plenty of room for it and the microfilm, when safely fixed, allows the toothbrush to do its job.

The use of talcum-powder boxes, cigarette lighters and a Chinese scroll as hiding places, have been described in various spy trials. But these are only a few of the countless hiding places employed. Others often in use are shoe soles and heels, toothpaste tubes, fountain pens, belts, book-covers, clothes-brushes, hair cream or ladies' make-up containers, keys, hollow coins, cigarette boxes, bottle corks and many many other everyday articles.

To ensure that spies cannot be unmasked through the amateur preparation of a microfilm's hiding place, Gaczyna pupils are taught to sole and heel shoes, to take apart brushes and clothes, to rebind books, drill holes in bottle corks and to restore them all without anyone suspecting that they have been tampered with.

Rule yII-B[1] recommends every Soviet Resident Network Operator abroad to 'avoid direct communication with informers and sub-agents'. But the inhabitants of Gaczyna are taught how to recruit informers, because Secret Service Headquarters state that 'under special circumstances a Resident Network Operator cannot avoid direct communication with informers and sub-agents'. Cadets are therefore taught to take every precaution when meeting another member of their spy network.

The first lesson requires the pupil to assume she is being trailed by plain-clothes Intelligence officers while engaged on a mission. She must shake off the shadowers and proceed to her rendezvous only when she is certain she is no longer trailed. To make this part of the training realistic, the student spies are actually trailed throughout Gaczyna. A student who presumes she is safe when making for her rendezvous when she has failed to lose her shadower is confronted by the 'detective' and severely reprimanded.

Students learn how to approach a possible future informer. Instructors posing as English or American civil servants, scientists or technicians, act out being awkward and dangerous contacts. The students learn how to cope with unpredictable men and women in tricky situations and talk their way out of difficulty.

[1] This is the Russian sign. In English it reads VII–V.

Before students are drafted out to their new 'country of birth' they undergo a tough final examination lasting three weeks.

The Examination Board comprises specialists in every field who decide whether the cadet is now fit for work in the particular country, or if he or she needs more time at Gaczyna.[1]

The decision as to whether a student is fit to assume another nationality is made only by examiners who are ex-citizens of the country concerned, and who can detect whether general speech and pronunciation, manners and behaviour are correct.

There is no appeal against the decision of the Board. All other examinations on specialised espionage subjects are supervised by Russians who conduct all tests in English.

Students who have passed their final examinations remain at Gaczyna until Moscow is ready to transport them to their 'country of birth'. Months may elapse but the students must remain in Gaczyna's Western surroundings until the moment of their departure. Russia's Secret Service directors believe that for them to mix with their fellow countrymen again might disrupt their ten years of conditioning and training.

[1] According to Soviet statistics, in 1959 five male and two female students failed. Since then every future Resident Operator and special agent has been passed as classified 'suitable for overseas duty'.

6   Spreading the Net Wide

Gaczyna is Soviet Russia's most important spy school because the Soviet Secret Service considers the English-speaking world its greatest enemy! But it is by no means the only institution of its kind. The Russians consider *all* capitalist countries their enemies and are on guard against them.

In the West of the Soviet Union there is the spy school called Prakhovka. During the Second World War, when Hitler's *Wehrmacht* seized Byelorussia, Prakhovka was evacuated to comply with Stalin's scorched-earth policy. An emergency school was set up near Ufa, in the Bashkir Autonomous Soviet Republic, but Prakhovka returned to its original location when it was rebuilt in 1947.

Prakhovka lies some seventy miles north-east of Minsk, the capital of the Byelorussian Soviet Republic. Its 220 square miles extend to the border of the Latvian Soviet Republic. Like Gaczyna, the whole territory is sealed-off by State Security guards. Prakhovka trains master spies for Norway, Sweden, Denmark and Finland in the northern part of the establishment; the Netherlands in the south-west; Austria and Switzerland in the south; and Germany in the south-east. As in Gaczyna, each division is a duplication of a particular country, and the training of students follows the principles adopted at Gaczyna.

Stiepnaya, which lies about 110 miles south of Chkalov and stretches along the northern border of the Kazakh Soviet Republic, is a factory for producing spies destined to work in Latin countries. It has the French sector in the north-west; Spain in the north; Italy in the north-east; and Portugal, Brazil, Argentine and Mexico in the southern zone.

There are two other schools of the Gaczyna type—one for Asiatic and Middle East races, and one for Africa. These are Vostocznaya,[1] which lies about 105 miles south-east of Khabarovsk, and Novaya,[2] about ninety miles south-west of Tashkent.

None of these schools is as large as Gaczyna but each year they pass out a considerable number of master spies.

Moscow's Secret Service Headquarters also maintains an efficient Intelligence network in all satellite countries. The Soviet rulers do not trust their own Russian people, so it is not surprising that satellite comrades are trusted even less.

To obtain an exact picture of what is going on at government, industrial, scientific and public level in Russia's satellite countries, Moscow swamps them with Soviet resident spies who are thoroughly schooled in spy establishments like Gaczyna; their training rarely exceeds five years, however.

The largest of these schools is Soyuznaya, which was established in 1924 and turned out spies for the 'Little Entente'. After these countries were swallowed up by Russia, the spy tuition was directed at the 'People's Democracies'.

Soyuznaya—roughly the size of Prakhovka—lying about eighty-five miles south-east of Tula and about the same distance south-west of Ryazan, accommodates the following divisions: Czechoslovakia in the north-west; Poland in the north; Bulgaria in the north-east; Hungary in the south-west; Rumania in the south; and Albania and Yugoslavia in the south-east. Although Yugoslavia does not belong to the Iron Curtain bloc, Moscow considers this 'renegade country' as belonging within the Soviet sphere of influence.

Kytaiskaya—about seventy-five miles south of Irkutsk, near the Baikel Lake and Mongolian border—caters for China, Japan, Indonesia, Mongolia, Korea and other Asiatic countries. Only Soviet students of Asiatic origin are accepted for training here.

In every Red satellite country there are 'Special Task' training colleges which prepare Czech, Hungarian, Polish and other

[1] For Asiatic and Middle East countries.
[2] For Africa.

Secret Service agents for work abroad. These are not Gaczyna-type spy schools, but are similar to the Lenin Technical School, Verkhovnoye. Cadets from these institutions are sent to work in foreign countries under the cover of diplomatic immunity, attached to their national Embassy or Consulate, or to the United Nations Organisation in New York. Their work is insidious and they actively help the Soviet espionage network to spread its web wide.

7 Rita, an Unusual Variety Artiste

Knowing now how Soviet spies are trained, it is easy to understand how Russian agents work successfully for years in a foreign country without detection. Their extraordinary success is due to their unique training and to the abundance of money at their disposal.

Unlike Britain, the United States and other Western countries, where Parliament votes the amount of Secret Service expenditure, and where it is consequently impossible to conceal large sums spent on intelligence development, the Soviet Secret Service is under no economic pressure and anually spends millions of dollars, pounds sterling and other currencies. Soviet master spies spend freely and are not expected to render accounts, as long as they show results.

Many Soviet spies have lived so daringly that their exploits might have been invented by a fiction writer. True spy stories, like the following, might have been invented by any modern author.

In April 1954 a Soviet Embassy cipher clerk in Sydney, Vladimir Petrov, and his wife Yevdokia, defected to the West. They were rescued from Soviet escorts, who were returning them to Russia, by Australian Security officers. The grateful Petrovs exposed the Soviet espionage network in Australia and disrupted the activity of the Soviet Secret Service. Several independent Resident Network Operators who were completely unconnected with the Soviet Embassy and the other exposed espionage organisations continued to transmit messages to Moscow. But the meagre information that got through to Soviet Secret

Service Headquarters was neither detailed nor adequate.

To repair the damage caused by Vladimir and Yevdokia Petrov, Moscow set out to establish a new espionage network. Woomera was a fast-growing research station for guided missiles and
nuclear development. There was no time to waste. Gaczyna-
trained Secret Service agents were sent to Australia. But the
Australian counter-intelligence was acutely spy conscious and any
new face in the area was automatically suspect. Moscow's agents
reported it would be dangerous to attempt to establish another
spy network, so Soviet Secret Service directors decided to wait
until tension had eased. Moscow Secret Service reports reveal that
some of these newly appointed resident spies in Australia remained
inactive for nine months before they dared to begin operations.
Meantime they found jobs, knowing that people with money and
leisure easily draw unwanted attention.

One of the new spies placed in Australia was Rita Elliott.
After an acclimatisation period of three months she'd created a
perfect cover for herself.

Rita Elliott was Esfir Grigoryevna Yurina, born in Moscow in
1923, the daughter of a circus artist, Grigoriy Ivanovich Yurin
who, in the thirties, joined Moscow's State Circus. Her mother
was a noted trapeze artiste.

Esfir was recommended by her Party Organiser as 'suitable
for special foreign service' and in 1943 was sent for special schooling. In 1945 she attended Gaczyna, the ace spy school for resident
operators in the English-speaking world, where she was entered
as A-450110/215-G, and from the day of her arrival was known
as Rita Elliott.

Her instructors decided the occupation of variety artiste would
be an ideal cover for her future work abroad and at Gaczyna
Rita perfected a circus act as a tightrope walker.

Despite her daily hours of acrobatic practice, Rita studied hard
and gained top marks in all her subjects. One of her progress reports, transmitted to Moscow Secret Service Headquarters,
stated :

'. . . This student has extraordinary abilities, not only as far as language is concerned but also in other fields of comprehensive schooling. She has the makings of a born agent and will come up to our highest expectations in her future career . . .

Her progress in language and general acclimatisation has no precedent. After only fourteen months she already speaks and behaves as if actually born in her country of adoption. All instructors are agreed that her accent is perfect . . .'

Rita passed her final examination at Gaczyna with honours. A few days later the Transport Department arranged her journey to Australia.

Rita Elliott was smuggled into Australia at the end of October 1955. She travelled to Adelaide where she remained eight days, acclimatising herself.

Her next stop was Melbourne. Her cover story was that she had come to find work, believing she had better chances there. She stayed at a respectable guest house catering for artists, spent a week getting to know Melbourne, and registered with a booking agent. She reported to Moscow :

'I registered for employment. He arranged an audition and was impressed by my performance. We signed a contract. He is confident he will place me shortly.'

Rita's next message to Moscow stated she had performed in Melbourne and had been well received. Her artistic career eventually took her to Sydney, Canberra and other leading Australian cities.

Once she was established, Rita stepped up her espionage activities. In a comparatively short time she set up a widespread spy ring and soon she was transmitting coded high-speed messages and sending microfilms of secret documents to Soviet Secret Service Headquarters. She concentrated on obtaining nuclear and other top-secret information. Assisted by go-betweens, she met government officials and influential people who had first-hand knowledge of work in progress on the Woomera range and in research centres.

Her method of obtaining information from people who under normal circumstances would have sealed lips seems too far-fetched even for fiction. But let me quote the authenticated wording of a Soviet Secret Service report about Rita Elliott :

'. . . Helped by her good looks she found it comparatively easy to attract men. After drinking with her in clubs they would accept her invitation to go to her apartment. There she plied her guests with drinks in which she had mixed a drug, temporarily converting them into a will-less object. She could then easily hypnotise the subject and suggest he was making a report to his superior. Expertly questioned, the man spoke freely and the tape recordings proved of utmost value.

The great importance of this method is that, before bringing the hypnotised subject back to normal, she orders him, on awakening, to forget everything that has been said, and to remember only that they were drinking together . . .'

The same report also suggests an alternative method :

'If a person is suitably drugged and ready to be worked on, the truth drug can be injected. In many cases this produces rich results.'

The report does not state if Rita Elliott also used this method.

Rita's ability to hypnotise her victims and extract top-secret information was by no means the only way she gathered information. And for nearly five years she worked to the complete satisfaction of her Moscow superiors without arousing any suspicions.

But despite her skill and far-sightedness, Rita could not forever escape the attention of Australian counter-intelligence. It was noticed that she entertained numerous influential men who were all, in one way or another, connected with nuclear research and secret work. Privately interrogated, these men insisted their association with Rita was social and personal. Each corroborated the others' statements that Rita never mentioned politics nor scientific research.

The Soviet Secret Service Control Agent in Australia, whose task it is to watch over the safety of independent Resident Network Operators, received a tip-off that Rita Elliott was under observation. At once, both Moscow and Rita were informed. But instead of recalling Rita, thereby giving the Australian authorities circumstantial proof that their suspicions were justified, Rita was instructed to 'abandon at once' all espionage activity and to order her sub-agents to remain inactive until further notice. Her radio and photographic equipment was removed to a safe place. Rita was told to continue her job as a variety artiste as if no change had occurred. Despite Australian counter-intelligence detectives keeping a round-the-clock watch on Rita, she managed to contact her informers and sub-agents, and to dispose of all incriminating espionage equipment.

Rita discovered the limpet microphones concealed in her home by Australian spy catchers but behaved as though she were ignorant of the security check. Counter-intelligence could pin nothing on her. Nevertheless, they continued their round-the-clock watch.

In view of this, Moscow saw no purpose in keeping her in Australia. So Rita Elliott—who was under surveillance merely because of circumstantial suspicion—was transferred to other duties.

In January 1961 'genuine' offers arrived for Rita Elliott from India, Pakistan, and other countries, tendering bookings in first-class variety and circus shows. Rita accepted, and in February 1961 left Australia.

Rita Elliott toured India but engaged in no espionage activities. She moved on to Pakistan and thereafter she simply dropped out of sight.

8 Eileen, a Quiet English Miss

One of the most sensational of women spies was Eileen Jenkins. She was a quiet unassuming spinster who emigrated from England to Canada and opened a small shop in Ottawa.

Eileen was so typically English that many of her Canadian friends and customers frequently joked about her Oxford-type behaviour. But she was liked and many a customer came to her little shop merely because of its 'so-English atmosphere'.

But Eileen was not English! Her true name was Tanya Markovna Radyonska. She was born in 1924 in Murmansk as the daughter of an O.G.P.U. (Russia's Secret Police) major. She had the 'right' background and so her Party Organiser considered her suitable for Secret Service work. At the age of twenty-one she passed all her qualifying exams and became 'Eileen Jenkins' when she arrived at Gaczyna. Her registration number was B-480822/039-G.

In May 1958, Eileen was smuggled into England and for nine days acclimatised herself to conditions in the United Kingdom. She spent most of the time in Carlisle.

She came to London, found lodgings in the King's Cross area and pretended to be seeking work as a shop assistant. But although she tried her utmost to find suitable employment she returned each day to her lodgings without success.

This was all preparation for her future plans. She was under orders from Moscow to stay in London without engaging in espionage; therefore creating a plausible reason for wishing to emigrate to Canada.

On numerous occasions she told her landlady and other lodgers that she was fed up being out of work while her savings dwindled. When she mentioned she was thinking of emigrating to Canada some encouraged her, but her landlady maintained that life was sweeter in England.

Eileen had been supplied by the third division of the Foreign Directorate in Moscow with Canadian 'relatives' and 'friends'. But Moscow warned her not to attract suspicion by forcing issues. So Eileen drifted along without a job, still pretending to toy with the idea of emigrating to Canada. But she did not waste these months in London. She learned to be more English than most English-born people. She made friends with office and shop girls who invited her to their houses. These invitations were rarely repeated because Eileen proved herself a bore and spoiled many a party. Her hosts had no reason to suspect her behaviour was brilliant acting. By nature she was a gay person, but her specialised work prevented her from developing close friendships.

Eileen Jenkins finally forsook her 'country of birth' and sailed for Canada where she arrived in March 1959.

She had no need to acclimatise herself to this new country. She was an immigrant. It was to be expected that she would be unaccustomed to the Canadian way of life. However, Moscow ordered her to await further orders before engaging in espionage. So she stayed six weeks in Montreal where she took a job as a saleswoman in a bakery. When she was ordered to Ottawa, the manageress tried to persuade her efficient saleswoman to stay, but Eileen invented an aunt in Ottawa who had fallen ill and who needed her at her side.

Eileen rented an expensive apartment in Ottawa where she spread the story of an aunt who had recently died and left her a comfortable nest-egg.

During her first week in Ottawa, Eileen recruited her first collaborator. She met him casually in a snack bar and soon discovered he was interested in meeting someone from England. She decided to use him, and in a microdot message to Moscow reported :

'I have found a nineteen-year-old junior clerk who works in a well-known firm. I have told him it is inconvenient for me to receive personal letters from Europe at my home. He agrees they can be sent to his address.'

The youngster had no suspicions and from then onwards microdot messages from Moscow were sent to Eileen through her new 'post box'.

Eileen was a good friend to the boy and frequently gave him presents. But she never recruited him for spy duties. In his employment he had no opportunity of gaining any secret information, and he was far too naive for go-between duties. Eileen preferred to use him as a 'post box' without his knowing that he was an important link in an espionage network.

Within four months of arriving in Ottawa, Eileen had successfully established herself as a master spy. Her greatest asset was her role as a typical Englishwoman in her middle thirties.

She devoted herself to charity work and was always eager to help anyone in need. Yet behind the scenes she not only operated an espionage set-up, but maintained a terror group, which kidnapped and murdered.

She ordered the execution of an electronics engineer who was born in Germany and worked in a Canadian armaments factory. She had tackled him as a potential informer and threatened him. If he did not provide her with information his relatives, who still lived in Communist East Germany, would be 'dealt with' for his lack of co-operation. The German foolishly retorted that he would tell the authorities of her threats, so Eileen arranged for him to be drugged and executed by her terror squad. His death was made to look like suicide.

Eileen also kidnapped and transported to Russia a Slovak immigrant working as a draughtsman in an aircraft design office. He also resisted her threats and tried to inform the authorities. He never managed to contact the police. While walking along the street, he was overtaken by a car, pulled inside and driven to an isolated country house. When transport was arranged, he was injected, and while unconscious, smuggled aboard a ship sailing to Russia.

By August 1959, Eileen had organised so many kidnappings and killings of 'elements who constituted a danger to the group' that Moscow became worried. Too-frequent deaths and disappearances could arouse suspicion. A Control Agent was sent to observe Eileen's activities and report on her.

Eileen was too well Gaczyna-trained to disobey Moscow's orders to go easy with her strong-arm tactics. But she continued to use blackmail and threats of violence in her recruitment of informers. Moscow did not interfere. She was transmitting more valuable information than any other Resident Network Operator.

Until July 1959 Eileen worked as a saleslady in a lingerie shop. But as her espionage network grew, her time-consuming job became a handicap. She decided to acquire a business of her own, and with the help of a business transfer agent soon found a shop in the same line of business. She was careful, however, not to use her 'cover' business as a meeting point for go-betweens, informers and sub-agents.

That Christmas, Eileen's life took a strange twist. An attractive man came to her shop seeking a suitable present for his mother. He liked Eileen and dated her. For the first time in her career as a master spy, Eileen allowed herself to become emotionally involved with another human being. But in January 1960, she discovered that her lover was a police official. She reported this to Moscow and received orders to continue her friendship and try to learn how much the Canadian authorities knew about Soviet espionage. Soviet Secret Service Headquarters recommended she should accept the police official's offer of marriage.

Eileen drained useful information from her lover, and from him heard about Igor Guzenko, a cipher clerk at the Soviet Embassy in Charlotte Street, Ottawa, who had decided to defect to the Canadians.

When Igor Guzenko finally decided to ask for political asylum in Canada, he was fully prepared for his break with the Soviets. He had listed a large number of documents which exposed a dozen Soviet diplomats in Canada who were engaged in most undiplomatic activities. However, it was essential that the highly confidential Embassy files, to which he had access, should not betray him if they should be spot-checked by a Control Agent. Therefore he left the documents in their files with their edges turned down so he could locate them swiftly when he needed them.

In the early hours of the evening of September 5th, Guzenko decided his D-day had come. He left the Embassy and went straight to the editorial offices of a newspaper, bearing sufficient documentary evidence in his pockets to put a dozen diplomat spies behind bars. But the editor believed the documents the cipher clerk presented to be forgeries. Editors are constantly being offered news stories backed by false evidence for which they are expected to make fabulous payments. Guzenko was shown the door.

Guzenko panicked. He had burnt his bridges and Soviet agents in Ottawa might already be searching for him. In desperation he went to various Canadian government offices and told numerous officials he wished to defect to the West. To his consternation, nobody would take him seriously. He was believed to be a 'nut' and his increasingly frantic insistence and agitation strengthened this belief.

But Guzenko was unwittingly aided by the Soviet Embassy. Alarmed by the inexplicable absence of the cipher clerk, the Chief Security Officer took emergency precautions. The door of Guzenko's apartment was broken down by unidentified raiders and his belongings were ransacked. The Canadian police were called to the scene, made a search for Guzenko and took him into protective custody. At last the defector could tell his story, show the documents he had stolen and be heard out without scepticism.

The Canadian authorities rejected the subsequent demand from the Soviet Embassy to surrender Guzenko on a 'capital charge', and granted him political asylum. Later it was admitted that Western counter-intelligence might well have remained in ignorance that the Soviet Embassy in Ottawa was the mainspring of an espionage network had Guzenko not defected.

When Eileen was told this story she scoffed at her lover. She performed a perfect piece of acting when she refused to believe the Canadian counter-intelligence had to depend upon information from a Soviet defector to unmask Russian spies. But her lover did not rise to the bait. Eileen had to report to Moscow that her fiancé 'either does not know or is too careful' to divulge Western counter-intelligence methods.

Eileen carried on her unique espionage activities until Moscow Secret Service Headquarters decided to change her country of operation. She received orders to leave Canada, the third division supplied her with 'genuine' letters from England saying her uncle was seriously ill, and her story was so plausible that her fiancé suspected nothing. He urged Eileen to leave without delay.

In which English-speaking country Tanya Markovna Radyonska has assumed a new identity is, as yet, unknown!

9   Mademoiselle Germaine

The case of Mademoiselle Germaine, as recorded in official files, seems like the creation of an over-vivid imagination.

Mademoiselle Germaine, a typical French woman, was not French. She was the daughter of a Rumanian father and a Georgian mother. The father, Soltan Cornescou, came to Odessa as a young man in 1913 because he hoped the busy Black Sea port would provide him with better opportunities than his own country. He found employment in shipping and a year later married Marfa Kalidze, daughter of the firm's Georgian manager.

In October 1916 a daughter—Irina Soltanovna—was born to the Cornescous. Irina, thirty-one years later, entered the Soviet Secret Service spy school of Stiepnaya as—Mademoiselle Germaine.

Irina's best subject at school was French, and it was arranged for her to enlist as a student at Moscow University, where she graduated in 1937 with a diploma in French.

Her first job was as French translator with the Publishing House for Foreign Languages, in Moscow. Soon she was transferred to work at the French department of the Moscow Radio Centre. Later, she was transferred to the French Section of the Comintern.

When the German-Russian war began in June 1941, Irina was posted to the Soviet Ministry for Foreign Affairs and became assistant to the head of the French Section. Her diplomatic career ended in 1945. When World War II ended Stalin decided to build up subversive forces overseas. Irina Soltanovna was earmarked for work in France.

Irina was put through Secret Service training at the Marx-

Engels School, and the Lenin Technical School. Afterwards, she had a period of 'assessment duties' at Moscow Secret Service Headquarters, and then attended the French-speaking division of the spy school at Stiepnaya. When she passed out as ready for espionage abroad, the forty-one-year-old (but much younger looking) master spy went to France as Mademoiselle Germaine.

After an 'acclimatisation' period in Paris she adopted the cover of a French governess. The only posts a Paris agency could offer were with a banker, which was a household where she might never come across any useful information; with a textile merchant in Lille, which she discarded for the same reason; with a businessman in Toulouse, which was too out of the way; and with a director of a Belgian steel concern, an equally unattractive post. Nevertheless, to establish her 'cover' as fast as possible, Irina accepted the job with the Belgian family.

Living with this family had drawbacks, however. It was impossible for Irina to keep espionage equipment in her room for fear of its being discovered. But having a substantial sum of money, as well as a list of people suitable for recruitment as agents and informers, she was soon able to find a hide-out for her technical equipment. She recruited sub-agents and set up her first espionage network.

To her delight the Belgian family proved to be an excellent choice as an employer. She was treated as one of them. They did a lot of entertaining and their guests included French and other West European industrialists, scientists, technologists, officers and even members of the Corps Diplomatique. So, quite fortuitously, Irina Germaine was soon able to pick up important scraps of secret information about vital industrial and political events.

After four months in their service, Germaine's employers decided they would return to live in Brussels, and suggested that she should accompany them. Moscow Secret Service Headquarters had assigned her to France and she could not change her assignment without consent. She transmitted a coded high-speed radio message to Moscow Headquarters and received permission to go with her employers to Brussels and establish herself there as a Resident Network Operator.

In Brussels her employers entertained as lavishly as in Paris, and, by using miniature 'limpet' microphones and wire recorders, Germaine often obtained and transmitted to Moscow Secret Service Headquarters information of great importance.

But this was only a fringe benefit. Germaine's main task was to set up an espionage network that penetrated Belgian military and research stations. This she did. Within six weeks of arriving in Brussels she had two spy webs operating and numerous agents and informers supplied her with blueprints, plans, military reports and other vital documents.

Her second-in-command, Paul Veken, was a Belgian who was apparently a fanatically religious office clerk. It seemed quite safe for Germaine to meet him whenever necessary. But despite her 'cover' and the precautions she took which stood her in good stead for many years, her association with Paul Veken eventually led to her exposure. She became complacent about their meetings in the park where she took her employers' children every day. She played ball with the children there and always chatted with Veken, who drifted along to share her park bench. It looked like a servant-girl romance. But they made a mistake that was eventually noticed. Veken never dated his servant-girl on her days off.

It was clever of Germaine to bring sandwiches to the park which she offered to Veken, but it was not so clever of him to eat only one and pocket the others containing microfilms. It was odd that Germaine and the children did not eat all the rich pastries Veken brought in exchange and that Mademoiselle always put some in her bag to take away.

Counter-intelligence agents, whose suspicions had been aroused, kept Germaine under observation and noticed these simple mistakes. She and Veken were arrested.

It was a 'scoop' for Western counter-intelligence. Not only was a master spy captured but most of Irina Germaine's espionage network of agents and informers were also rounded up, together with Russia's most recently perfected and secret spy equipment.

Another Russian master spy who operated successfully in France for many years was Pierre.

After seven years of spying in French Africa, Pierre, whose real name was Demyan Mironovich Sheykov, was ordered to leave Tunis and go to France where he linked up with the Soviet Resident Network Operator, Yvette. Pierre's task was to set up a supplementary spy web.

Pierre chose to become a Paris bus conductor—an occupation which enabled him to meet agents, informers and Yvette, without arousing suspicion. A bus conductor meets and talks to people all day.

Pierre carried on espionage in Paris for almost six years before he betrayed himself.

An alert Security officer happened to notice the same bus conductor buying an expensive brand of chocolates on a number of occasions. This was out of character for a bus conductor and on a hunch the agent trailed Pierre. He learned that Pierre always bought the chocolates in the centre of Paris, travelled to a suburban apartment and, an hour or so later, returned across the city with the chocolates to meet his girlfriend. Yet Pierre seldom stayed long at the girl's apartment, and they *never* went out together.

A secret visit was paid to the girl's apartment while she was out. Several boxes of chocolates were found with only two chocolates missing from each box. In each case it was the same two types of chocolates!

Pierre and Yvette were kept under observation until counter-intelligence knew enough to make an arrest. The two spies were caught red-handed with a box of chocolates. Two of these chocolates contained . . . microfilms.

10   Maria and Marianne

The Kremlin's policy is to keep West Germany in a permanent state of a war of nerves, hoping the West Germans will decide to accept Russia's 'solution to the German problem'. To foment unrest the Soviet Secret Service maintains a large apparatus of Resident Network Operators in the former *Reich*. The Kremlin knows what makes the heart of the Federal Republic of West Germany tick, and aims to increase its tempo.

Russian-born spies, thoroughly trained at Prakhovka and with assumed German identities, operate not only in West Berlin, but also in the American, British and French sectors of West Germany. The West German and Allied authorities are well aware of this and employ a strong force of well-trained spy catchers. But although many minor Communist spies are arrested and brought to justice, the German and Allied counter-intelligence rarely trap a Soviet master spy.

But Maria Knuth was a Russian master spy who did not get away with it.

Maria Knuth was a trained Soviet agent who passed herself off as a German actress and who lavishly entertained American and British officers at her luxurious apartment in a suburb of Cologne. For many years her spy network supplied Moscow with secret reports, details of military strategy and airfield construction, the composition of the West German police and frontier guards and the military plans of the West German Army.

One of Maria's major agents was Inspector Hermann Westbold of the Frankfurt-am-Main police. He was an officer whom the Allies trusted implicitly. When finally arrested Westbold confessed he had been a Soviet agent for several years and had been paid 'at least £45 per month' for his services.

Maria Knuth was trapped by M.I.5 agents in the central Post Office in Cologne. Documents in her possession at the time of her arrest were said to have 'greatly shocked' Allied military commanders. Four other members of Maria's espionage network were also arrested and a powerful short-wave radio receiver-transmitter, together with other valuable espionage equipment was seized. But the rest of Maria's spy web were alerted, went underground and escaped arrest—among them Maria's 'superior' whose identity was never established.

The case of Marianne gives a typical picture of how Soviet Secret Police Resident Operators work in West Germany. And Moscow Secret Service Headquarters consider Marianne to have been one of their most outstanding spies in West Germany.

Marianne arrived in Frankfurt-am-Main in May 1958. She was Nadiezhda Mikhailovna Makaryeva, born in Kharkov in 1925, and the daughter of a Russian Trade Union Organiser. At the age of twenty-one, while studying economics at Moscow University, she was recommended by her Party Organiser as being 'suitable for special training'. Like all Soviet Secret Service agents, she underwent the usual training routine and was eventually transferred to Prakhovka, where she enrolled in the division for Germany as Marianne Koch—G-472903/018-P.

After ten years at Prakhovka, she passed her final examinations with top marks and was sent to East Berlin. In April 1958, she slipped quietly into the Western Sector of the former German capital. Her identity papers showed she came from the American zone of West Germany to West Berlin and her cover story was that she was on a visit.

Moscow Secret Service Headquarters chose West Berlin as Marianne's first stepping stone to setting up a spy network in the American sector of the city. She spent several weeks acclimatising herself to life in West Berlin, and meanwhile studiously refrained from engaging in any espionage activity. But she was not idle. She memorised all the Allied sectors of the city and reported

C

that she 'felt at home'. She soon decided which of the numerous restaurants and night-clubs would be good meeting places for her collaborators.

She was an attractive blonde and many men tried to date her. But Marianne reserved her feminine charm for the influential men she intended to meet.

Marianne travelled to Frankfurt-am-Main and established herself in a modern apartment block. She set up a Secretarial Service Bureau that, as well as being a 'cover', served as a post-box and a meeting place. She also undertook photostating and industrial photography which justified her keeping photographic equipment on the premises.

Hiding behind this respectable façade, Marianne got down to business. She studied the background of the Germans on her list of suitable recruits and selected those who had previously been connected with the Nazi movement as her first target. They were men with all the necessary qualifications to become informers or go-betweens and who had a skeleton hidden in the cupboard.

In postwar West Germany, money was precious and Marianne combined blackmail with bribery. A few weeks after her arrival in Frankfurt-am-Main she recruited her first informer. He was a man in an influential position in a secret weapon research station department. Marianne rang him and made it clear it was in his own interest to come to her office. He kept the appointment and Marianne told him flatly that she wanted him to supply her with blueprints and documents of everything on his department's secret list. She said she'd pay well. The man reacted predictably. He was a German patriot who would not dream of spying for an enemy power and threatened to inform the police. Marianne gestured to the telephone. She too had something to tell the West German police and the U.S. authorities! She could prove he was working in Frankfurt-am-Main, using the identity of a dead man. He was an ex-Nazi wanted for crimes against humanity. 'So go ahead and telephone the police,' she added coolly. Her victim struggled but she pinned him down mercilessly with a dossier showing his pre-war Nazi record. The victim surrendered.

Once again money was discussed and the very next day Marianne received the first of many, many blueprints and documents from him. A day later a microfilm copy of it was on its roundabout way to Moscow Secret Service Headquarters concealed in the handle of a shaving brush. Time proved this first recruit to be Marianne's most valuable informer.

Within six months of her arrival in Frankfurt-am-Main, Marianne was controlling a vast network of informers, go-betweens and special agents. Her radio receiver-transmitter was always busy and her 'work shop' industriously produced and despatched micro-filmed blueprints and documents, as well as microdot messages. She concentrated on obtaining information about West German installations but she also spread her web to the American sector in West Germany. Moscow Secret Service Headquarters soon confirmed that 'the information from U.S. sources in West Germany is of great importance as a supplement to news from West German sources'.

Marianne's energy was unflagging. She extended her spying activities to West Berlin where she again established a Secretarial Service Bureau in a respectable tenement block. Spying in West Berlin was more rewarding than in Frankfurt-am-Main, because numerous experienced agents could easily slip in from the Communist sector of East Berlin.

Marianne's successful espionage network in West Germany carried on for many years, working with clockwork precision. It functioned so smoothly that Moscow finally decided it could be controlled by a less valuable master spy. Marianne was recalled to the Soviet Union to 'engage in new duties'.

Moscow Secret Service Information reports have recently made no mention of Marianne and it can be concluded she has been given a new identity and is working in the field . . . somewhere.

11   The Scandinavian Beauty
from Leningrad

Greta Nielsson's cool, proud Scandinavian beauty; her flaxen
hair and smiling, violet eyes would have earned her top fees as a
cover girl for magazine photographers. Film directors would have
made her a star because to her charm and acting talent she could
have brought a high standard of intelligence, thus providing a
rare combination of beauty and brains.

But Greta had no desire for the limelight, nor for public ac-
claim. Instead, she devoted her talents to commerce. She rented
premises in the heart of Copenhagen, supervised the décor and
opened a gift shop which, within only a few weeks, was flourish-
ing and prosperous. Its success was undoubetedly due to Greta
Nielsson's charm and personality which secured her satisfied
customers and a contented staff.

Greta spoke Danish like a native, although it was sometimes
possible to detect a foreign inflection in her voice. But this was to
be expected. Greta was Swedish by birth and had lived all her
life in Göteborg until romance and a Danish husband had brought
her to Copenhagen. She'd adapted swiftly to the Danish way of
life, but after the 'sad event' in her life, had decided to continue
to live in Copenhagen. The 'sad event' was the desertion of her
husband. There had been another woman and a baby on the way,
it was rumoured, but Greta's friends did not press her for details.
It was obviously painful for her to talk about it. Thus, Greta and
her gift shop enjoyed the goodwill and hospitality of the Danish
people, who had no suspicion that both were the traitorous in-
struments of a foreign power.

Greta was probably one of the most successful women spies of his decade. Not only did she carry on her espionage for twelve long, unsuspected years; but when her espionage activities finally became known, she evaded arrest under circumstances that cast serious doubts upon her guilt.

Greta Nielsson was not Danish, not even Swedish. She was Russian, and the Soviet Resident Network Operator of an efficiently spun spy web at the heart of which was the seemingly innocent gift shop.

Greta Nielsson's true name was Valentina Nikolayevna Malinovska. She was the daughter of a Leningrad Party Organiser. Because of her 'immaculate Bolshevik background' and her fanatical devotion to the Communist cause Valentina was excellent material to further the Soviet cause. Her intelligence and beauty were taken into account when she was selected for espionage training. She was drafted to the Soviet spy school Prakhovka in October 1944. On admission to Prakhovka, Valentina Nikolayevna Malinovska assumed a new identity. She became Greta Nielsson—of Swedish nationality and born in Göteborg. She was officially registered as Soviet Secret Service Agent, Code Number O-441610/011-P.

Soviet spy schools are thorough and it was ten years before Valentina's tutors were satisfied she could enter Sweden and be accepted as Swedish born and bred. But meanwhile, Valentina had studied hard and had become expert in all the techniques of modern espionage. When she passed her finals at Prakhovka in November 1954, she was thirty-one years old. She was classified as thoroughly qualified to assume the part of Resident Network Operator ... in Denmark!

Greta Nielsson was held in reserve for some time at Prakhovka. The Director of Moscow Secret Service Headquarters' First Division (the section responsible for obtaining 'identities of genuine foreigners' and 'providing Soviet Secret Service agents with aliases') was not entirely satisfied about her cover documents. He ordered a thorough check to ensure the future spy's safety. The final report he received was that Greta's cover was foolproof.

After ten long years of training, one more Soviet spy was ready to go into action.

Two weeks before Christmas 1954, Greta was smuggled into her 'country of birth'. For a month she 'acclimatised' herself to Sweden, travelled widely to familiarise herself with the country, and used her spy training to learn if she had aroused the suspicions of zealous counter-intelligence officers. During this 'acclimatisation' period she obediently observed the strict Soviet Secret Service rule that forbade her to engage in espionage activity of any kind.

Some weeks after her arrival in Sweden, Greta travelled to Copenhagen. There she married a Dane, on orders from the Director of Moscow Secret Service Headquarters' Third Division. Her 'husband' had been carefully chosen and vetted by Moscow's Secret Service Selection Board. He was an ardent Communist fellow-traveller who was fanatically dedicated to Moscow's ideology. For years he had posed as a respectable and devoutly religious businessman while subversively furthering the aims of the Red Fifth Column. He eagerly obeyed Central Committee's orders to give Greta the legal right to Danish nationality through marriage.

Soon after Greta was married, her husband conveniently disappeared. It is now known that Russia's Transport Department skilfully whisked him out of Denmark and into the U.S.S.R. There he was awarded a post as Language Tutor at the Prakhovka Spy School under control of the K.G.B.

Greta was now established as a Danish citizen, with full legal privileges, and quite free of the restrictions imposed on foreign residents. The Danish authorities never at any time suspected Greta's marriage was arranged by Moscow, and the only dubious comment made about Greta was surprise that her husband had been so stupid as to desert such a beautiful and charming woman.

Moscow Secret Service Headquarters provided Greta with substantial funds to establish a front and create an espionage network. Everything Greta did had to stand up to possible investigation, so she could hardly establish a business unless she could show the source of her capital. Greta turned her personal attributes to good account. She contrived to meet well-to-do Danish businessmen and used them ruthlessly. Trading with her sexual charm she convinced these dupes to provide her with the capital she needed to launch her gift shop. They happily left the running of the business to their charming manageress, and in return were content with the favours she secretly but sparingly permitted them. By the unscrupulous use of sex, Greta provided herself with a legitimate source of capital and influential friends of good social standing.

Once the gift shop façade was established, the spy network could be constructed. Moscow provided a list of persons suitable for recruitment, Greta interviewed them personally, sounded them out and built up a corps of agents and informers. Simultaneously she supervised the secret installation of technical espionage equipment in her gift shop. She worked so efficiently that by March 1955 her espionage network comprised seventeen fully operational agents and informers; microdot messages and microfilms were flowing to Moscow Headquarters and her Soviet Secret Service superiors were so impressed that frequent acknowledgements of her 'exemplary good operational work and far-sighted ingenuity' are recorded in M.V.D. Reports.

Greta took care not to be personally involved in espionage field activities. The Prakhovka Spy School had taught her how some incautious Soviet Resident Network Operators in other Western countries had been detected and arrested after disregarding the paramount Soviet Secret Service security rule *never* to gather vital top secrets personally. Greta was the director of an efficiently functioning espionage network and was determined its safety would not be endangered by a foolish disregard of basic precautions.

Greta concentrated on gathering information about NATO installations, their striking power and other military and technical top secrets. Her secondary objectives were inner-circle secrets involving economic and political strategy. Her hand-picked agents and informers, who occupied key positions in the Danish administration, provided her with a steady flow of factual information that was invaluable to Moscow.

Microfilms of classified blueprints, diplomatic documents and secret reports were concealed in cleverly constructed and innocent-looking containers. Gift shop clothes brushes, electric shavers, alarm clocks, elegant compacts and a wide variety of similar articles flowed out of Copenhagen in the luggage of passengers travelling by scheduled airliners, on trains or boats. They contained vital top secrets destined for Russia's Secret Service Headquarters. Urgent messages and reports to Greta's superiors were transmitted in code by high-frequency shortwave radio. In addition, countless microdot communications, concealed under postage stamps on picture postcards, were mailed to cover addresses throughout the Western world. Secrets were relayed to Moscow's Secret Service Directors in scores of ways.

Greta soon reached a working arrangement with her Soviet Secret Service counterpart in Stockholm, who was in turn in close contact with the spy, Colonel Stig Wennerström. Their working arrangement was not authorised by Moscow, but their private scheme enabled the two Resident Network Operators to exchange useful information and increase the factual evidence they could send on to their superiors. In this way they both improved their personal standing with their Moscow directors. Spies are always eager to please their masters; they live dangerously and a dissatisfied director can dispose of an inefficient operator easily by 'leaking' about his spying activities to the interested authorities, or by even more ruthless means. Assassinations of Soviet spies by K.G.B. 'execution squads' is not unknown.

The gift shop was never at any time under suspicion. Its beautiful manageress was regarded as a good and respectable citizen. Her go-betweens, the links between Greta and her agents, passed off as casual customers. The basis of Greta's success was that the go-betweens *never* handled incriminating evidence. Nor did they receive on-the-spot payment for their services. They merely whispered a verbal message to Greta or were told what instructions they should pass on to an agent. Microfilms and payments for services rendered were always left in ingenious 'dead-drops' and were collected only when it was safe to do so.

Colonel Stig Wennerström was arrested in June 1963. At once an intensified spy-hunt was launched in Sweden and the other Scandinavian countries. But no spy-link to Greta's gift shop was discovered. Nevertheless, Greta wisely decided that the increased vigilance and the tightening up of the cooperation between Scandinavian, American and British counter-intelligence experts might bring one of her many agents under suspicion. She immediately forbade go-betweens to visit the gift shop and introduced a safer method of communication. 'Dead-drops' were henceforth used for all forms of contact. Go-betweens, agents and informers received their instructions through the Press. An advertisement reading : 'Darling, please come home, I miss you terribly, Karin', would instruct Agent A that his orders and payment were to be collected the next day from his 'dead-drop' O1 at Fiolastraede in Copenhagen. When Agent A collected his coded instructions they would include the wording for Greta's next advertisement. And when Agent A inserted the pre-arranged advertisement : 'Anita, lunch usual place arranged Wednesday, bringing Olaf, Carl', in the same newspaper, Greta would know that a microfilm containing NATO secrets was to be recovered from 'dead-drop' O2 at Copenhagen's Loevstraede. The prearranged code was changed for each advertisement, and different newspapers and journals were used by different agents.

For vitally urgent messages the telephone was used. Greta took every precaution with the telephone and used the 'black box'. This is a security apparatus designed by the Moscow Secret Service Headquarters' Technical Division for the protection of their agents working in foreign countries.

Greta rented an office under an assumed name and asked for two telephones with different numbers to be installed. She gave one number to her agents for telephoning urgent messages in prearranged code, and kept the second number secret. She hooked up both telephones with the 'black box'. When she was due to receive a call from an agent, she dialled her secret number from a public telephone. The agent dialled the number of the other telephone and contact was made through the 'black box'. This had an automatic timer that disconnected the call after a few minutes. Counter-intelligence agents need at least seven minutes to trace any call and by this security measure Greta protected herself from all risk of telephone tracing. The 'black box' instantly disconnected both telephones if anyone entered the room in which they were installed. Greta never visited the premises where the 'black box' operated and always called her secret number from a different public callbox.

Greta's efficient espionage organisation continued its treacherous activities for four years after Colonel Stig Wennerström's exposure in Stockholm. It inflicted considerable damage upon Western security and defence. Its collapse after twelve years of unsuspected treachery was brought about by circumstances over which Greta had no control.

The detection of Angela Maria Rinaldi's Soviet Secret Service Network in Rome in 1967[1] proved the existence of Russian spy rings in other Western countries, including Scandinavia. Security probes were intensified but Danish counter-intelligence was unable to trace any evidence of any Soviet espionage network. Nevertheless, they had been alerted and remained on the lookout. Then a high-ranking K.G.B. officer defected to the West and brought with him documentary evidence of the Soviet espionage networks in the free world. One of them was Greta's spy web.

But even while Allied counter-intelligence experts were sifting the defector's information, Moscow's alerted Secret Service Transport Department had begun rescue operations. Greta was whisked away to the Red capital and her agents received 'May-Day' signals. They destroyed all incriminating material and went into hiding. Greta's technical espionage equipment was destroyed.

When Allied spy-catchers raided the gift shop they found no evidence that it had been used for espionage. And although Greta had disappeared, there was no sound reason to believe she was a spy. A picture postcard addressed to one of her wealthy pro-

[1] See pages 77–81.

moters arrived from Cairo. Greta apologised for her impulsive departure which was a spur-of-the-moment decision. She hinted she might not return to Copenhagen because she was contemplating marriage with an oil Sheikh. This was mildly sensational news but not impossible. Greta had been on extremely friendly terms with an Arab millionaire throughout his stay in the Danish capital.

But Greta's spying activities were exposed by one of her agents who unwittingly played into the hands of the spy-catchers. Fearing that the 'dead-drop' where he had concealed his microfilm camera, codes and other spy equipment was under surveillance, he did not retrieve and destroy them. Counter-intelligence stumbled upon this 'dead-drop' and found the agent's special 'working orders'.

'Gerda, darling, pining for you. Carl', meant: 'Contact spy leader in devised safety manner.'

'Will the lady to whom I gave a lift in my Volkswagen last Friday night and who gave her name as Gerda, please communicate with me', meant: 'Deposit material at Dead-drop O3.'

The special 'working orders' were lengthy. They were not only the private code for inserting and understanding advertisements; they also provided for any emergency that might arise in the course of everyday espionage work. Yet although Allied counter-intelligence agents broke down the code it was of no practical value beyond proving that a spy web had been operating in Copenhagen. Greta's safety precautions were so sound that the 'working orders' gave no lead to the identity of even one solitary Russian agent; nor were the Allied spy-catchers able to lay hands on the agent whose spy tools they had captured.

The exposure of Greta Nielsson's, alias Valentina Nikolayevna Malinovska, ultra-efficient espionage network was classified at Moscow Secret Service Headquarters as 'an unfortunate but unforeseeable disaster for which no blame whatsoever can be attached to the Resident Network Operator in Copenhagen'.

What was even more important for Russia was that a brilliant and veteran spy had successfully eluded arrest and, after a well-deserved rest, could be assigned to 'other duties'.

Since no man, or woman, is infallible, Greta Neilsson or Valentina Nikolayevna Malinovska may well be heard of again, headlining newspapers as a detected spy. But it will be with a different identity!

12   Angela, the Red 'Tsarina'

In March 1967, the revelations about a spy ring operating in Italy shook the Western world.

As more news leaked out, with arrests and deportations of suspected agents, the people of the free world were stunned to learn that the spy web had been working on the European continent and in the Mediterranean area for thirteen years, supplying Moscow Secret Service Headquarters with priceless NATO secrets. Many people were astonished to learn that the leader of this espionage network was the attractive Italian artist-parachutist Angela Maria Rinaldi.

But let us go back to the beginning.

In 1954, Moscow Secret Service Headquarters decided that the thirty-eight-year-old Angela should become the Resident Network Operator of a spy web in Italy. She was intelligent, energetic and pretty. She looked fifteen years younger than her actual age and was 'respectable'. The Soviet espionage directors were confident she would succeed. They were right.

It did not take the methodical Angela long to set the espionage machinery in motion. She was equipped by Moscow Secret Service Headquarters with lists of people suitable for recruitment, and went about her task skilfully and with sufficient funds to pay her agents and informers handsomely. By the spring of 1954 her first espionage network was fully operative and her Secret Service superiors in Moscow were pleased with the regular flow of secret information she transmitted.

One of her agents was her husband, the Italian parachute ace, Giorgio Rinaldi. He did not know that his pretty wife was almost fifteen years his senior. He believed she was a year younger than he : the entry in her parachute-club membership card confirmed her 'age'.

Giorgio Rinaldi, who had access to NATO and other air bases as an instructor, used ultra-modern photographic and film techniques for taking pictures of secret bases as he flew over them to prepare his exhibition jumps. Whenever he had the opportunity to talk with 'men in the know' he recorded every word with his concealed hair-wire recorder. He also microfilmed important blueprints, documents and plans whenever the opportunity arose.

Angela, who was nicknamed by her agents 'The Tsarina', transmitted to Moscow Secret Service Headquarters all the information, microfilms and recordings she received from her husband and from other agents in Italy, Greece, Cyprus, Somaliland, Morocco, Spain, Portugal, Switzerland, Scandinavia, England, Turkey and Africa. Some of the information was transmitted to Moscow Headquarters by coded high-speed radio broadcasts; other messages were in invisible ink and reached Moscow *via* roundabout routes. Microdot communications were affixed under postage stamps on picture postcards or business letters and microfilms and recordings were concealed in innocent-looking containers.

'Dead-drop' or pick-up spots also played an important role. Angela was extremely clever in choosing her 'dead-drops'. Her pick-up spots at Turin Zoo, the one near the Basilica of Superga (burial place of Italian kings), and those in and near Rome, on lonely mountainsides or in busy city centres in Switzerland, were such perfect hiding places that no one ever discovered them. And the 'medieval village' in Turin's Valentine Park, which had been set up to serve as a laboratory for processing films, was a unique idea.

In 1956—two years after Angela created her first successful spy ring in Italy—Moscow Secret Service Headquarters summoned her husband, Giorgio, to the Soviet Union to receive training in general espionage methods. Giorgio could not travel to the U.S.S.R. without Italian and Allied counter-intelligence being alerted, so a clandestine trip was arranged. He flew secretly from Paris to Russia, without his journey being recorded in his passport. At the end of his short training course he returned to Paris by the same route, without arousing suspicions in France or Italy.

Shortly afterwards, however, Italian Security began to keep an eye on Giorgio when he became friendly with a Soviet Army officer. Angela was warned by the network's Control Agent of the danger, so Giorgio stopped meeting him. After months of unfruitful round-the-clock trailing, counter-intelligence was satisfied that Giorgio's meeting with the Soviet Army officer had been a harmless encounter. The watch on him was called off.

During the next seven years neither Angela, her husband, nor any of her agents and informers came under suspicion. Meanwhile, a continuous supply of important strategic secrets flowed unhindered to Moscow Secret Service Headquarters.

In 1963 counter-intelligence once again became suspicious of Giorgio. The Rinaldis' antique shop, which was Angela's espionage 'cover', appeared to be in financial difficulties, yet Giorgio still seemed to have plenty of money. A close watch was kept on him, but so discreetly that Angela's control agent did not learn about it. The ceaseless shadowing of Giorgio yielded no results but counter-intelligence doggedly continued the watch as though sensing they would meet with success.

Eventually security agents learned Giorgio had made a secret trip from Paris to Moscow. This was their first rewarding discovery. Giorgio could have been arrested and charged with illegal travel, but counter-intelligence held its hand. They wanted evidence to connect him with espionage. If Giorgio believed he was safe he himself would provide the required proof. He did this by making more illegal air trips to the Soviet Union and thus tightened the noose around his neck.

In mid-March 1967 the spy-catchers' long wait was at last rewarded. When Svyetlana Stalin arrived in Rome—after having defected in India and requested political asylum—Angela Rinaldi received a coded high-speed radio message from Moscow asking her to 'locate the dangerous traitor and kidnap her'. Moscow's orders were transformed into action. All agents and informers including Angela, her husband and their chauffeur-agent, Armando Girard, sought to trace Svyetlana while she hid in Rome on her flight to Switzerland. When it was learned that Stalin's daughter had flown to Berne, Angela decided she must be kidnapped there.

By this time not only Giorgio but Angela and Armando too were under constant surveillance. Unaware of any danger, Armando Girard was arrested on the Italian-Swiss border as he was crossing into Switzerland. He was in possession of microfilms of American air bases in Spain.

Counter-intelligence promptly arrested Angela Maria and Giorgio Rinaldi in Turin. They seized an ultra-powerful shortwave radio receiver-transmitter and code books, microfilms of NATO bases in Italy and U.S. bases in other parts of Europe, and a large quantity of specialised espionage equipment.

Giorgio broke down and gave away several secret 'dead-drops'. For four days counter-intelligence agents kept them under surveillance. On the night of March 20th, 1967, a black Soviet Embassy car, occupied by Yuriy Pavlenko (an attaché at the Soviet Embassy in Rome) and his wife Natalia, stopped at one of these secret hiding places in the Via Braccianese, in suburban Rome. As Pavlenko thrust his hand into the 'dead-drop' and pulled out a roll of microfilm, Security men pounced. Pavlenko ran to his car. But two police cars pulled across the road, front and rear.

Protected by diplomatic immunity, the Soviet attaché was safe from arrest; all the Italian authorities could do was declare him persona non grata and expel him and his wife from Italy. Two days after the detection the three left Rome on a Czechoslovak airliner. Angela Maria, Giorgio Rinaldi, and Armando Girard were officially charged with espionage and eventually received long jail sentences.

The exposure of 'The Tsarina's' espionage network had far-reaching consequences. In Cyprus a Soviet Embassy attaché, Boris Petrin, and a Soviet airline employee, Nikolai Renov, were deported for complicity in the espionage. Two Cypriots were arrested and accused of spying on British and U.S. installations. One of the Cypriots, a telephonist, Vikention Boutros, handled

overseas calls to embassies; the other, David Shehabin, worked
on a R.A.F. base in Nicosia. In Greece a Soviet agent was arrested
in Athens, and in Switzerland it was officially announced that
'the possibility of arrests cannot be excluded'. In Rome it was
disclosed that counter-intelligence had leads to Angela's operators
in Scandinavia, France, Spain, Morocco and elsewhere. Many
arrests followed.

13 Women Spies with Almond Eyes

Those in the free world who discuss 'Red Spies' usually have in mind the Soviet Russian espionage networks. Those more familiar with Communist espionage include in this term the lesser known, but equally dangerous, intelligence networks maintained by Russian satellite countries—Bulgaria, Czechoslovakia, East Germany, Hungary, Poland and Rumania. But few people are aware of Mao Tse-tung's well-organised and highly efficient Red Chinese Secret Service.

Until recently Communist China's espionage activity in the free world was not taken seriously by American and European experts. They believed that the Red Chinese Secret Service concentrated its intelligence service on targets in Asia, and did not think Red Chinese espionage constituted an imminent danger to Western countries. But in recent years this neglect of the danger of Red Chinese espionage has enabled Peking's spies in America and Western Europe to penetrate into these target areas without hindrance.

The foundation-stone for Red Chinese espionage was laid nearly forty years ago. During the twenties Stalin foresaw that China would become a Communist country and an ally of the U.S.S.R. Acting upon Lenin's theory, 'the sooner efficient and effective Bolshevik intelligence cadres are established in as many capitalist countries as possible, the more rapid will be the development of world revolutions,' Stalin ordered, 'our Chinese comrades must be trained in Secret Service work'.

The spy school Kytaiskaya was established, and Secret Service trainees were selected from hand-picked Chinese Communists who had been sent to Russia to attend the Lenin School and the Eastern University. Stalin's trusted Secret Service chief, Colonel Mikhail Nikolayevich Yakubovsky, was placed in command of the Chinese spy school where, in the early thirties, some three hundred Chinese Communists received schooling in every field of espionage.

After Mao Tse-tung became head of the Communist government in Kiangsi in 1934, and after Li Li-san (the hero of the Canton insurrections against General Chiang Kai-shek) had gained control of important territory in war-stricken China, the flow of Chinese Communists to Russia increased. Both Mao Tse-tung and Li Li-san realised that schooled men and women were urgently needed for developing the future Communist China. Those cadets, classed as suitable for Secret Service work, were sent to Colonel Yakubovsky's spy school Kytaiskaya.

When Mao Tse-tung and his comrades succeeded in transforming China into a Communist country, an independent Red Chinese Secret Service Headquarters was set up in Peking, organised on the same pattern as Moscow Secret Service Headquarters. The directors of the various Directorates at Peking Headquarters were students from Kytaiskaya who had passed through the spy school with special honours. But they were as yet insufficiently experienced to control a world-wide espionage system, so Moscow Secret Service Headquarters supplied them with expert 'advisers', who directed the newly created Red Chinese intelligence network.

A number of spy schools, organised on the lines of Kytaiskaya, were established in Red China and considerable numbers of trusted Chinese Communists were trained annually. But the original institution in the U.S.S.R., Kytaiskaya, was still used for turning out Chinese master spies. Only after the ideological rift between Khrushchev and Mao Tse-tung deepened did the training of Chinese spies in Russia cease. All Red Chinese Resident Network Operators are now trained in Communist China.

Peking's main intelligence target is Generalissimo Chiang Kai-shek's stronghold, Formosa, and substantial numbers of Red Chinese spies have been smuggled into the island.

Since the mid-fifties hundreds of Red Chinese master spies,

sub-agents and informers—among them a great proportion of women—have been arrested in Formosa. They had obtained reports, plans, blueprints and other top-secret documents from Chiang Kai-shek's highest military circles, political and economic advisers and from the Generalissimo's headquarters.

As soon as the danger of Red Chinese espionage was recognised, Nationalist China's counter-intelligence and Security forces were substantially increased. But, although it seemed that Chiang Kai-shek's swift action had curbed Red Chinese espionage in Formosa, it was not the case. Peking had succeeded over the years in smuggling ever increasing numbers of spies into Nationalist China. Despite the considerable number of arrests made, the flow of vital secrets to Peking Secret Service Headquarters steadily mounted.

Nationalist China is by no means the only target of Peking's intelligence. Indonesia, the Philippines, South Korea, Vietnam and many other countries in the Far East are also subjected to Red Chinese espionage. Blackmail is commonly used to extort funds for financing Peking's agents and many examples of Red Chinese agents' blackmail activities are known in the U.S.A., and particularly in San Francisco.

Another target for Red Chinese espionage is Hong Kong. Since Mao Tse-tung seized power in China an immense number of Red Chinese spies of both sexes have been arrested by British counter-intelligence. And to show how efficiently Peking Secret Service Headquarters operate, I shall describe here one amazing case of spying that was discovered.

For security reasons the Hong Kong authorities did not release all the information they learned about this dangerous Red Chinese espionage ring—most of the evidence was heard in camera. But it was disclosed that 'this massive spy ring was engaged in sending information to Communist China. Radio messages from spies have been intercepted and tape recordings seized by the police.'

It was also disclosed that fashionably dressed women in expensive cars played a leading part in the spy ring. Counter-intelligence officers, who kept one woman under secret round-the-clock sur-

veillance, caught her in the act of handing a Chinese messenger-
boy a banknote which contained microdot messages giving the
name of a hotel frequented by a senior Hong Kong police officer.
Other microfilms seized contained 'secrets of vital importance
to a potential enemy'.

The danger of Red Chinese spies to American officials in South
Vietnam was revealed in the following report which a U.S. security officer in Saigon sent to his superior :

'American officials living here are unwilling to employ new
housemaids for fear they are giving spies free access into their
homes.

Documents seized by Security officers in South Vietnam show
100 girls have been trained as spies by instructors from Peking
and have been ordered to seek work with American families. The
girls, aged from seventeen to twenty, were chosen by Red Chinese
training officers for their beauty and education, and their aptitude
for English.

In the same spy-training camp sixty miles north of Saigon those
girls with long hair had it cut off to look "more presentable", and
discarded their traditional Vietnamese full-length gown with long
silk trousers for the simple Western dress as worn by girls in Saigon. The girl-spies were told to "pilfer documents from your employers, carry out general espionage and assassinate your employers if you are ordered to do so".'

Whether it is Hong Kong or Vietnam, India or Pakistan, Korea
or Laos, or any other Far Eastern territory, the archives of prac-
tically every Asian country contain volumes about unmasked Red
Chinese spies and their espionage networks. These same records
show the rapid increase in the number of new Red Chinese master
spies entering Far Eastern countries with perfect 'cover' identities. An unusually large proportion of these spies are women.

Up-to-date reports about Red Chinese espionage in America,
Western Europe, Africa, Australia, New Zealand, Japan and
other countries of the free world reveal that Peking Secret Service

Headquarters have declared 'war without weapons' on the non-Communist world. Recent arrests of spies in Germany, the Benelux countries, Switzerland and many other territories have revealed that these men and women were in the employ of Red China.

Mademoiselle Louise Mainard (who was arrested while passing on copies of highly confidential political documents) broke down and confessed she was working for Red Chinese intelligence.

The beautiful night-club hostess of high repute, Kimi, acted as Red Chinese Resident Spy Operator in Tokyo for eight years. But only when her espionage network was detected, and its thirty-four agents and informers arrested, was it proved that Kimi had supplied Peking Secret Service Headquarters for some eight years with blueprints, documents and other data on Japan's defences, secret weapons research, science, technology, strategy and economy.

Fräulein Alma Gruber, who was arrested while in possession of a microfilm containing top-secret information, admitted the microfilm was destined for Peking Secret Service Headquarters.

These instances illustrate that Peking Secret Service Headquarters do not rely only upon Chinese nationals for espionage in Western countries. Most of the agents and informers in the employ of the Red Chinese chief Resident Spy Operators are foreign fifth-columnists and fellow-travellers who are not known as Communists in the country of their birth. They infiltrate into Ministries, organisations and research centres, gain access to secret information and supply their Red Chinese spy chiefs with the material they require.

During the comparatively short time Mao's spy webs have been fully operational, case histories indicate that Red Chinese master spies are as efficient and as dangerous as their Soviet Russian colleagues. The following case of Lily-Petal is a striking illustration of the cunning and efficiency of the world's youngest espionage web—Mao's 'army without uniforms'.

14   Lily-Petal

On a hot afternoon in June two years ago, New York police answered a homicide call and sped to a modest Chinese restaurant on the waterfront called the Chop-Suey. A grisly scene confronted them. Amidst the bloody chaotic disorder of the ransacked premises the body of a beautiful Chinese woman lay upon the corpse of an elderly man. Both had been stabbed to death.

The police investigated methodically. The murdered Chinese woman was identified as Lee Yan-sung, the graceful proprietress of the Chop-Suey restaurant, whose Oriental charm had won her a large clientele and whose excellent dishes ensured the satisfaction of her patrons. She was known as Lily-Petal, a name which accurately symbolised her graceful and delicate beauty.

The murdered man was Wang En-ping, an elderly uncle who assisted Lily-Petal to run her business. He was kindly, courteous and well liked by his many customers who bought ready-to-take-away Chinese food in sealed containers that he sold over the vestibule counter.

The neighbourhood was shocked by the tragedy.

It seemed evident the two victims of violence had surprised thieves in the act of robbing the restaurant. Checking systematically, the Homicide Department consulted the Narcotics Squad, as well as Crime Prevention detectives. It was thought their files might yield clues to any unsavoury characters who had been associated in any way with the Chop-Suey. It was learned that from time to time the Narcotics Squad had made spasmodic raids upon the Chop-Suey restaurant in pursuit of illicit drugs. But this was not unusual. All premises on the waterfront came under narcotics surveillance. All that these raids had proved was that the restaurant was strictly law-abiding. Experienced law officers had officially classified the Chop-Suey as 'all clean and above board'.

Neither Lily-Petal nor her uncle had made enemies and the police attempted to find the thieves by tracing the property they had stolen. Weeks passed and the investigation became routine. Months elapsed and the murders at the Chop-Suey restaurant became just one more unsolved crime.

Yet for a time the investigating officers had come close to exposing a crime far more sensational than murder. That they did not do so is not to their discredit. They lacked knowledge of two essential facts. (1) The dead woman was *not* the true Lily-Petal. (2) The dead man was *not* her uncle. But to discover this, the officers would have needed to go back in time sixteen years. Had they done so, they would have proved themselves much shrewder than the F.B.I. and the British Intelligence Service, both of which had been brilliantly duped.

It is now known that for more than a decade and a half the Chop-Suey was the headquarters of a Red Chinese espionage network in the United States.

On a cold October night some forty years ago, in the squalid Chinese tenement quarter of Chicago, Ho Yan-sung's teenage wife was suffering the agony of childbirth. When her pains had eased, she smiled down happily at the little wrinkled face of her new-born baby who would be named Lee Yan-sung. But the young mother did not live to see Lily-Petal flower. A few days later she died of childbirth fever.

Life was not easy for the widowed Ho Yan-sung. He could not afford to take time off from work to look after his baby daughter and gratefully accepted the offer of kindly neighbours to take care of little Lee. He had loved his wife deeply and was determined to provide their daughter with a good home and a safe and secure future. He worked the hardest and the longest hours at the laundry.

Time passed, and as Lee grew into a delicate young beauty Ho Yan-sung saw the reincarnation of his beloved wife. Hard

work and good fortune enabled him to improve his way of life
and the squalid tenement block background faded into an un-
pleasant memory.

Ho Yan-sung worked tirelessly and saved assiduously. Eventually he bought a shop which he made prosperous with unflagging industry. Ho Yan-sung's fortune flourished. He and Lily-
Petal now lived well and he was content he had kept faith with
his long-dead but still beloved wife. Only one ambition had still
to be fulfilled : to return with his daughter to the land of his fore-
fathers and search out any of his once numerous family who still
lived.

When Lee became twenty-one, Ho Yan-sung's birthday present to her was the news that they would embark for a prolonged
journey to the Far East. He planned to be away from Chicago
for three months. The honest Chou Hsien-foo, who was his friend
and capable assistant, could be trusted to take good care of the
business in his absence.

Lily-Petal and Ho Yan-sung sailed happily to Hong Kong,
unaware that they would never again see the land of their birth.

After a week exploring Hong Kong, Ho Yan-sung learned
that a relative might still be living on the Chinese mainland. With
some difficulty because of political problems, he finally persuaded
a junk skipper to sail him across.

What fate overtook Ho Yan-sung and his daughter, Lily-Petal,
is shrouded in mystery. It may be that their junk was overwhelmed
and sunk by a fierce storm that suddenly sprang up, or they may
have died in some other way. What is certain is that their bodies
were taken ashore by the crew of a Red Chinese gunboat, and it
was officially reported that the drowned corpses had been found
floating in the water.

Whatever the true facts may be, Red China *made no report*
of the incident to the Hong Kong authorities, although passports
found on the bodies clearly established them to be citizens of the
United States.

Peking Secret Service Headquarters carefully examined the
Yan-sungs' American passports and other documents which they

received from the Secret Police. They decided good use could be made of them. The identity of Lee Yan-sung could be assumed by a trained Red Chinese agent. Personality records were consulted and Agent Min Chiau-sen was selected for the hazardous assignment of impersonating Lily-Petal.

Min Chiau-sen was a fully fledged master spy, scheduled for work as Resident Operator in the United States. A convincing 'cover' background for her had already been painstakingly fabricated. But the possession of Lily-Petal's passport and other personal documents provided the Red Chinese with a ready-made authentic background . . . if only Min Chiau-sen could pass herself off as Lily-Petal.

'There are physical differences between the two women that can't be disguised. Also, Min is five years older than the dead girl,' worried the Director of the section controlling espionage in America.

'Min Chiau-sen is two centimetres taller,' admitted the Director of the Operational Division. 'But Lee Yan-sung is young and could still grow a little. Also, Min is physically fit and doesn't look her age. She'll pass.'

'But they don't even *look* alike,' objected the Director of the American Section. He handed his colleague two photographs. 'See for yourself.'

'When Min changes her hairstyle it'll make all the difference,' the Operational Director decided. 'Europeans are so unobservant that to them, all we Asiatics look alike.'

The Director of the American Section was not convinced. He proposed Min's photograph should be substituted for Lily-Petal's in the passport. But his colleague objected strongly. The American Authorities had means of detecting forgeries, he insisted. If they discovered anything wrong, Min's new career would be finished before it began. There was a risk, yes. But if Min succeeded in passing herself off as Lily-Petal, it was a risk worth taking.

Clever make-up artists worked delicately on Min's features, giving subtle touches to her eyebrows and lips, and rearranging her hairstyle. Almost magically Min soon bore a convincing like-

ness to Lily-Petal's passport photograph. The ultimate decision
was made, Min was given a final detailed briefing and conveyed
to Hong Kong.

On her arrival at the British Crown Colony, Min Chiau-
sen, who was now and in future Lee Yan-sung, boldly confronted
the authorities. She was a good actress and had rehearsed her
part thoroughly. With tears glistening in her beautiful eyes she
sobbed out the story of the drowning of her beloved father, and
of the callous ill-treatment she'd suffered at the hands of the Red
Chinese who had rescued her from the sea. The officials were
deeply moved by the girl's distress and offered her every help and
comfort.

'You're lucky they permitted you to return to Hong Kong at
all,' said one.

'They took all they could from me first,' said Lily-Petal bitterly. 'All my father's money and valuables, my wristwatch and
jewels, and even a gold locket with my mother's photograph.'
She opened her handbag. 'Look! All they've left me is ten dollars, my return ticket to the States and my passport!'

'If you are destitute, we can...'

'Thank you. I can manage. I have travellers cheques at the
hotel. They'll keep me in Hong Kong until I get a boat back to
the States.' She choked back a sob. 'I'll be travelling alone . . .
now.'

Lily-Petal's act was so convincing that her story was swallowed
whole by alert officials who were constantly suspecting trickery.
This was reassuring to the spy. If she could hoodwink the Hong
Kong authorities, who were well versed in the subtleties practised
by spies to penetrate the British Crown Colony's security,
she had every hope of deceiving the United States immigration
officers who would have no reason to harbour any suspicions
of her.

Lily-Petal went to the hotel where the real Yan-sungs had
stayed, and where her deception would be put to a more severe
test. But both the head porter and the manager, who saw an end-
less chain of arriving and departing guests, persuaded themselves

they recognised her. Lily-Petal repeated the story of her tragedy and they believed it unhesitatingly.

Lily-Petal had overcome the biggest obstacle of all. She had even deluded people of her own race who were not as blind as Europeans to Asiatic features.

In the seclusion of her hotel room that night, Lily-Petal wrote a glowing report to the Director of the Peking Secret Service Headquarters, using a memorised code. The following morning she sent it by ordinary mail to a Hong Kong cover address from where it was transmitted to Red China.

Lee Yan-sung had gained a second face.

Lily-Petal entered the U.S.A. without a hitch. But she dared not 'return' to Chicago. Peking Secret Service Headquarters could obtain no information about the dead Yan-sungs' Chicago background. If Lily-Petal returned to her father's shop, a close friend or relative would see through the impersonation. Lily-Petal instead went to New York where she rented a modest apartment and, on Peking's orders, consulted a lawyer to have her father's affairs wound up. The lawyer suggested a trip to Chicago so that the Estate could be settled speedily, but Lily-Petal resisted the proposal. She sobbed that she could not bear to return to her once happy home, with its poignant reminders of a cruel tragedy.

While the lawyer established that Ho Yan-sung had left all his savings and property to his daughter, Peking scheduled Lily-Petal for the customary acclimatisation period. During this time she was not allowed to engage in any espionage activities; instead she familiarised herself with life in New York. This continued until her lawyer had sold her father's business to the assistant, Chou Hsien-foo. When Lily-Petal received her inheritance it provided legitimate funds with which she could invest in a Chinese restaurant—the Chop-Suey.

Peking had provided Lily-Petal with a list of likely people to recruit as espionage agents and informers. They were ideological sympathisers, men greedy for money, or the victims of blackmail. All the necessary technical equipment for the setting up of an efficient espionage network was secretly installed in the Chop-

Suey and a large sum of hard cash was placed at Lily-Petal's disposal. Wang En-ping, an experienced master spy with a bona fide cover, was appointed her assistant. He posed as her uncle.

Soon, Lily-Petal had recruited a large ring of agents and informers, none of whom were Asiatics. Lily-Petal was too efficient to arouse the suspicions of the authorities by associating too often with Orientals.

From the outset the Chop-Suey restaurant was an efficiently functioning Red Chinese espionage centre. The dining section at the rear of the premises was an ideal 'post-box'. Agents and informers unobtrusively dropped microfilms of classified blueprints and secret reports into empty cups or bowls when Lily-Petal cleared away the dirty dishes. The counter in the vestibule, where Wang sold ready-to-take-away Chinese food in sealed containers, provided the 'pay-off'. After depositing their microfilm with Lily-Petal, the agents stopped at the counter to buy Chinese food to take home. In the sealed container was secreted the spy's reward : never less than a thousand dollars, in low denomination bank notes.

The astute Soviet Secret Service Control Agent in New York discovered the secret of Lily-Petal's Chop-Suey restaurant. He dutifully informed his Moscow superiors. In due course he was ordered to recruit Lily-Petal for the Soviet Secret Service. He gave the task to the infamous Colonel Rudolf Ivanovich Abel—Russia's most important Resident Network Operator in the United States of America, and without doubt one of the most able master spies in the history of world espionage.

Spies have a pressing need to satisfy their masters with their work. They also speak the same language and Colonel Abel had no difficulty in coming to terms with Lily-Petal, who had no qualms about double-crossing her own people. Colonel Abel was given access to all microfilms of top-secret blueprints and other vital documents before Lily-Petal transmitted them through her own secret channels to Peking Secret Service Headquarters' 'American Section'. Colonel Abel kept his part of the bargain by supplying Lily-Petal with vital secrets received from his own agents. Peking was delighted with the wide scope of Lily-Petal's espionage network and frequently praised her for 'excellent work of unique importance', never suspecting she was a Sino-Russian double agent. Colonel Abel too profited and basked happily in Russian approval of his spying efficiency. Thus do spies prosper!

Lily-Petal's secret partnership had other advantages. Colonel Abel helped Lily-Petal introduce a foolproof system of communications between herself and her agents that would save her from suspicion if the F.B.I. ever trailed or arrested one of her spies. He stressed the folly of keeping incriminating technical espionage equipment on the premises and Lily-Petal transferred it from the Chop-Suey to a safer hiding place. The value of Colonel Abel's advice was proved later when he was betrayed by Colonel Reino Hayhanen and was arrested by the F.B.I. Not one link between the Chop-Suey restaurant and Colonel Abel's espionage network was ever discovered or suspected. Lily-Petal was able to continue her highly efficient master spying activities for Peking Secret Service Headquarters for another ten years.

Lily-Petal never slackened her security measures and indeed continuously revised them. Neither the United States Security Services nor the F.B.I. ever had, at any time, any suspicions that Lily-Petal was a master spy. Her successful espionage might well have continued another sixteen years had she not been exposed by the idle whim of an old man.

One sunny day in May two years ago, an aged Chinese hobbled into the Chop-Suey restaurant and before sitting down, stared around as though hoping to see somebody he knew. Lily-Petal hurried over to him to be of service.

'I am looking for Lee Yan-sung who owns this restaurant,' the old man said.

A sixth sense warned Lily-Petal. She asked cautiously: 'You have business with her?'

'I am Chou Hsien-foo. I bought her father's business in Chicago. She knows me well. We are old friends.'

It was a tense moment for Lily-Petal. This sharp-eyed old Chinese had known both Ho Yan-sung and his daughter well.

She dared not try to deceive him. She made a split-second decision and said sweetly: 'I am *so* sorry. A few days earlier and you would have been lucky. But Lee Yan-sung has just gone away for a long vacation.'

'When will she return?' Chou Hsien-foo asked anxiously.

'In a month or so—perhaps even three. She'll let us know.'

The old man's face showed his disappointment. 'I can't stay that long in New York.'

Lily-Petal became aware that a regular patron sitting at a nearby table was listening, although he pretended to be engrossed in his newspaper. He must have heard her lies. Spies are always on their guard against possible F.B.I. investigators and this particular customer had already aroused Lily-Petal's suspicions. Hurriedly, almost rudely, she ushered Chou Hsien-foo into her private study at the far end of the dining room.

'You must be my guest,' she told the old Chinese. 'I will have a special dish prepared for us.'

'It is not customary to be invited by a lady,' Chou stammered in embarrassment.

'I am Lee's best friend,' Lily-Petal reassured him. 'She would wish me to make you an honoured guest.'

Lily-Petal was able to lull any suspicion the old man may have had, and when he left she had quite recovered her confidence.

But not for long. Wang told her a regular patron had left a message that he'd call back that same evening to discuss a private matter with her. It was the same man who had listened to her conversation with Chou Hsien-foo.

The lives of spies are unenviable. Every move they make is fraught with danger. For sixteen years Lily-Petal had lived in a constant state of nervous tension. Her fear of arrest magnified even innocent actions into menacing threats to her life and liberty. She believed that at long last the F.B.I. were on to her and feared she would be taken to Police Headquarters and grilled relentlessly. Lily-Petal cannot be blamed that after exposing herself to unceasing strain for so long, her nerve finally snapped.

Lily-Petal panicked. She decided to go into hiding and find her way to Hong Kong, from where she could return to Peking

Secret Service Headquarters. She possessed a specially prepared passport for use in emergency and all the ready cash she would need.

But Lily-Petal made a fatal mistake. She ignored the stringent rules of procedure laid down by Peking Secret Service Headquarters' Operational Division. She neglected to obtain official permission to abandon her post, and even failed to warn Wang of the impending danger. She simply fled.

Believing that Min Chiau-sen had defected to the 'hated American Imperialists', the Operational Division at once ordered an all-out manhunt for the vanished master spy.

The truth about Min Chiau-sen's fate cannot be established because the precise details about her end are locked away in the files of Peking's Operational Division. But it is known that three weeks after Lily-Petal's startling disappearance, she and Wang En-ping were found stabbed to death in the Chop-Suey restaurant.

Is it too far-fetched to assume that special agents of Peking's Operational Division found Lily-Petal's hiding place, transported her back to the Chop-Suey and set the stage for apparent murder by thieves? Wang En-ping was doubtless suspected of conspiring with Lily-Petal and shared her fate.

The Chop-Suey restaurant no longer exists. But if Lily-Petal's numerous agents now work for some other Red Chinese master spy, established somewhere in the United States of America, remains an unanswered question.

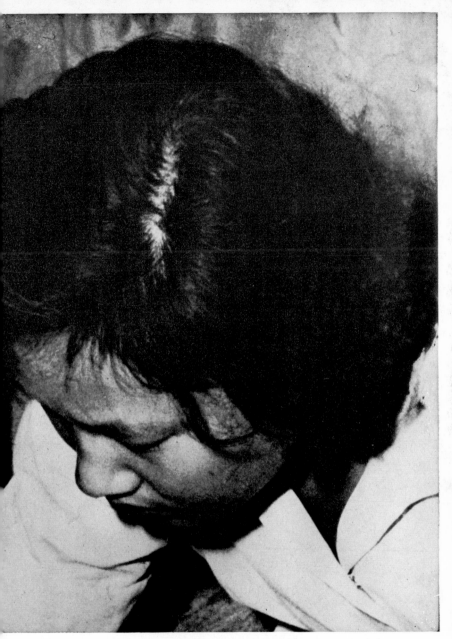

1. The Red Chinese master spy Min Chiau-sen who worked in New York for many years. Masquerading under the identity of the dead Lee Yan-sung, she became known as Lily-Petal, and from her Chinese restaurant at New York's waterfront regularly supplied Peking Secret Service headquarters with vital information—until her activities were brought to an untimely abrupt end.

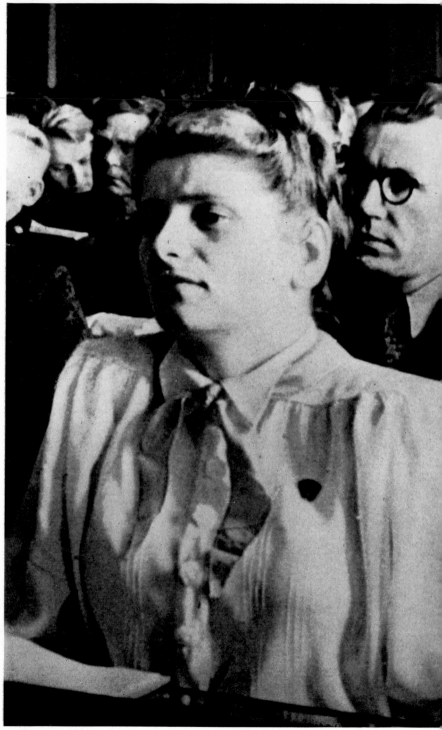

2. Greta Nielsson—the Scandinavian beauty from Leningrad. But the so typical Scandinavian proprietress of a Copenhagen gift shop was—Russian! She had been transformed into a Scandinavian in the Soviet ace spy school Prakhovka.

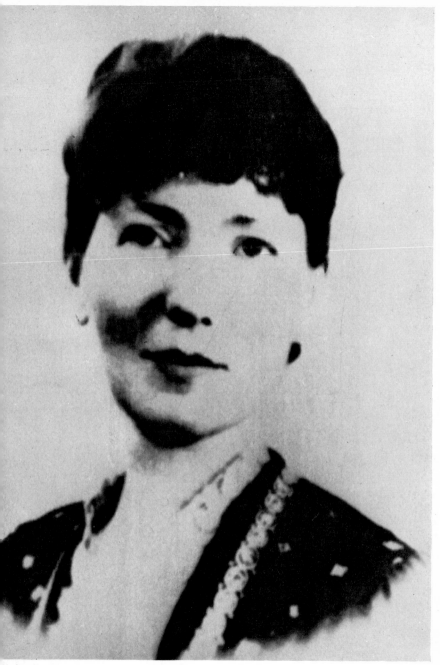

3. Angela Maria Rinaldi—the Red 'Tsarina'—was an admired Italian artist and parachutist who was held in considerable esteem. But under the cloak of respectability he was the leader of a widespread espionage network in Italy and supplied Moscow Secret Service headquarters regularly with priceless N.A.T.O. secrets. The Red Tsarina's' exploits as a spy merit the description of being 'stranger than fiction'.

4. Italian ace parachutist Giorgio Rinaldi—husband of Angela Maria. Whilst flying over secret military and N.A.T.O. bases and installations on his way to give exhibitions on parachute jumps he would take pictures with miniature cameras and other ultramodern equipment, which his wife passed on to Moscow Secret Service headquarters

. Maria Knuth, a thoroughly trained Soviet master spy, was posted as a German ctress and for several years supplied her Soviet Intelligence directors with secret eports, plans and documents on military dispositions in West Germany. Here she is ictured huddled in a chair in a High Criminal Court; she had had a heart attack and ad been allowed to attend court resting in a chair.

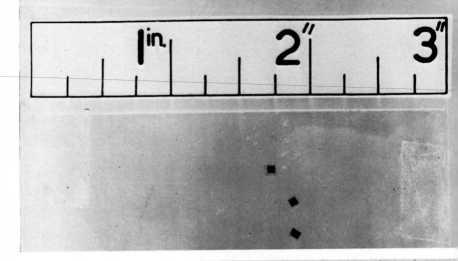

6. Microdots. This is what they look like and how tiny they are. For trained master spies it is easy to conceal microdots under postage stamps and send them through the ordinary post to 'cover' addresses on their roundabout way to Moscow or Peking Secret Service headquarters.

7. One of the microdots has been enlarged and the word message is clearly legible.

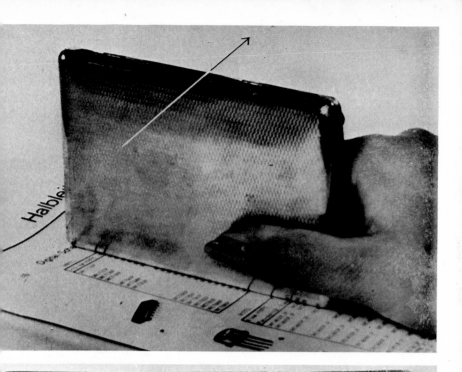

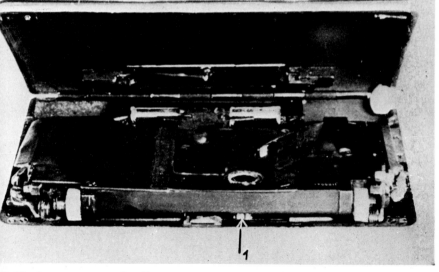

8. The latest type spy microfilm camera—not larger than a cigarette case.
(Top) The spy presses the camera against the document and moves it slowly across it.
The procedure is repeated until everything has been photographed; when developed,
the microfilm strips are stuck together and the whole document can be enlarged to its
original size.

(Above) The same type of microfilm camera opened. It shows the rolling, lighting
and other mechanism.

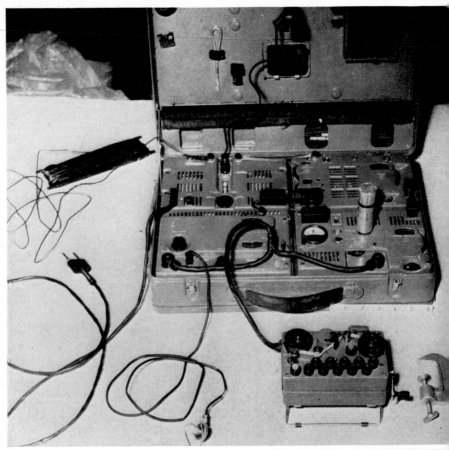

9. (Top) A radio transmitter powerful enough to send coded espionage messages to Moscow or Peking Secret Service headquarters. The small gadget beneath is a tape-keying device.

	Дни недели	1-я передача		2-я передача		3-я передача		Позывные
		Время ГМТ	Частоты КГЦ	Время ГМТ	Частоты КГЦ	Время ГМТ	Частоты КГЦ	
I	Среда	0528	5325	0558	5829	0628	6487	3-8-2
II	Понедельник	0515	5266	0545	5778	0615	6562	9-0-5
₃	Вторник	0504	5508	0534	6386	0604	6935	6-4-7
IV	Понедельник	0520	6822	0550	7548	0620	8129	1-0-8
V	Вторник	0509	6947	0539	8073	0609	8815	4-9-2
VI	Четверг	0501	7461	0531	8546	0601	9332	5-8-1
VII	Четверг	0531	7827	0601	8864	0631	10081	7-2-9
VIII	Вторник	0517	6643	0547	7666	0617	8711	2-4
IX	Вторник	0533	6473	0603	7488	0633	8172	8-0
X	Понедельник	0526	5147	0556	5812	0626	6764	9-2
XI	Пятница	0529	5656	0559	6255	0629	6907	6-5
XII	Вторник	0415	5221	0445	5744	0515	6881	

10. (Right) Soviet code-key recently captured by Western Counter-Intelligence agents.

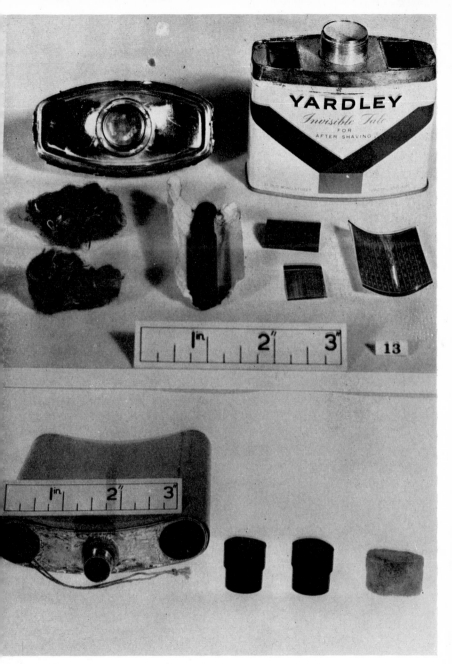

11. The torch, the Yardley bottle and the container below were provided with false compartments for hiding microfilms. They were used by Soviet spies.

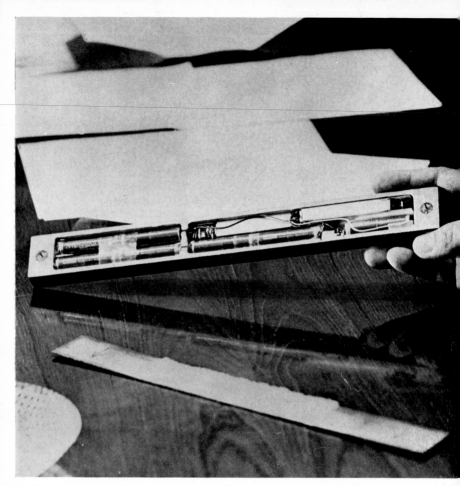

12. An electronic listening device, disguised as a piece of wood, which two Czecho-slovak diplomats attempted to get placed in the U.S. State Department, Washington, D.C. The device can transmit very-high-frequency radio signals and listen in on conversations in any room in which it is located. The device is a small rectangular wooden case which can be hidden easily.

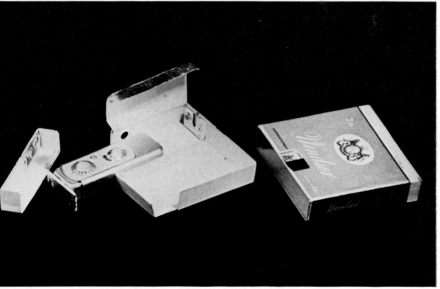

13. (Above) Three microfilm cameras frequently used by Soviet spies, and a cigarette box in which microfilms were hidden; it had a cleverly constructed secret hiding place.

14. (Below) Microfilm camera hidden in a cigarette box.

15. (Above) Captured Red Chinese microfilm which is shown here enlarged. It contained one of the exhibited code-keys.

(Below) A carved replica of the Great Seal of the U.S.A. which, presented by Russia, contained hidden microphones that enabled the Russians to overhear every word spoken in the American Ambassador's study.

16. (Top) Side view of one of the many microphones which were buried in the wall of the United States Embassy in Moscow and had, for many years, been betraying confidential conversations of American diplomats to Soviet Secret Service headquarters.

(Above) One of the probe tubes in the wall of the American Embassy in Moscow.

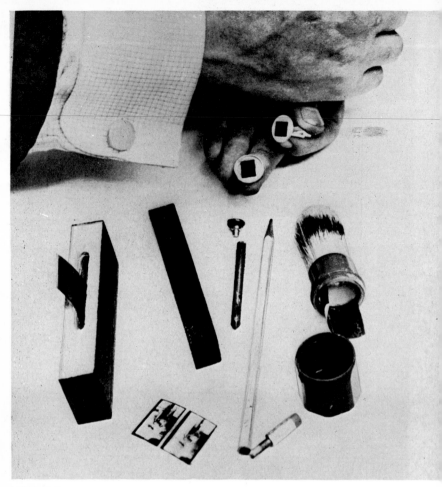

17. Tools of espionage.
Soviet spies use hollow shaving brushes, hollowed out nails, pencils, cuff links to hide and transport microfilm messages. Sometimes they bungle; these microfilm containers were seized by F.B.I. agents.

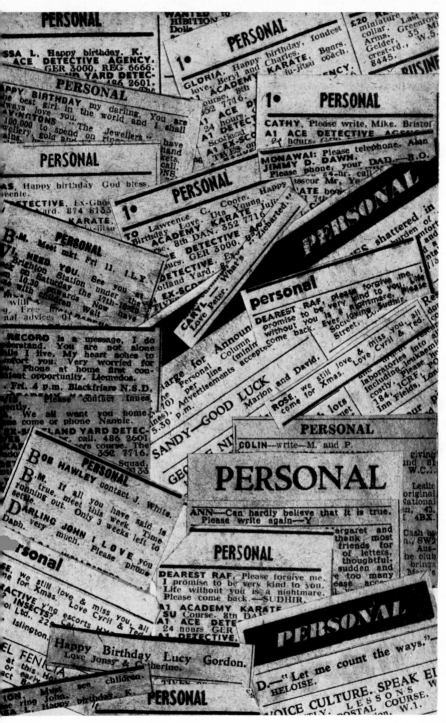

18. Ingenious methods of communication.

Unusual advertisements in the personal columns in British newspapers which could well be secret 'private code' messages.

ASSOCIAZIONE NAZIONALE PARACADUTISTI D'ITALIA

Sezione Provinciale di Torino

Medaglia d'Oro V. M. Mario Giaretto

Cognome **ANTONIOLA**   Nome **ZARINA (RINAL**

Nato a **Torino**   Provincia

il **5.8.928**   Socio **Ordinario**

Distretto Militare di

Residente a **Torino**   Provincia

in **Corso Svizzera 137**   n°

Telefono n° **251669** Professione **pittrice**

tuato corso n°   dal   al

enze al corso n°   su   comportamento

rendimento

to esame

r i militari: ha prestato servizio dal **dicembre 1944** al **maggio 1945**

esso **X° C° Armata Germanico (Rep. X mas.Nuotatori Par**

n il grado di **capomanipolo** in qualità di **ausiliaria**

19. (Top) Russian diplomat Yuri Pavlenko with his wife and son. Pavlenko was arrested whilst taking a microfilm from one of the Rinaldi 'dead-drops'.
(Above) Angela Maria Rinaldi's Italian National Parachute Association identity card

15 Red Women Spies are Everywhere

Red women spies are operating in every country of the free world, even in tiny principalities like Liechtenstein and Monaco. The more secret information culled from all over the world, the easier it is for Intelligence officers to deduce a coherent pattern of military and diplomatic intentions.

The successful espionage agent must forever remain unheralded. The spy who excels is the one whose name is never known; the spy whose fame, or infamy, is publicly acclaimed has failed. Those Russian women spies who are known to the West, and whose case histories have been described in the previous pages, have proved themselves self-sacrificing, skilful and efficient. Their proficiency in their chosen profession cannot be denied, but that they are known at all is a black mark against them, and raises the question :

How many Red women spies are so good at their job that the West will never know of them?

Probably a great many. Red women spies have been a big headache for Western counter-intelligence as is shown by the preceding and following espionage case histories.

Pamela Mason lived in New York and daily rode the subway to the skyscraper block where she sharpened her pencils, took dictation and typed her boss's letters. She was a mousy, frumpish young woman, much too prudish and introverted to appeal to men. Yet her wide-eyed awe when she listened to boasters encouraged them to entertain her and bask in her adulation. Pamela was never 'with it' or 'in' on anything. She was a fringe-haunter, being invited to parties and receptions without anyone's being sure why she was there at all. She met diplomats, politicians,

D

scientists and research workers. But her special talent was in being 'ethereal', never attracting attention to herself, nor being in evidence.

Pamela was one of Moscow's master spies. During the many years she worked in New York she completely lost herself among the other millions living in that great city. She supplied Moscow with an enormous amount of off-the-record information.

It is to the great credit of U.S. Intelligence that Pamela Mason ever came under suspicion and was winkled out from her niche into which she fitted so snugly. But her detection put Western counter-intelligence to so much time and trouble that Moscow considered her services valuable on this score alone.

From New York to Tokyo—Red women spies are everywhere. Who would have suspected that the beautiful Japanese governess Kioni was a Soviet Resident Network Operator?

Kioni established herself in Tokyo in 1955, built up her spy ring while carrying on her duties as a governess, and was not unmasked as a master spy until the summer of 1963.

For eight years Kioni supplied Moscow with valuable information about Japan's defence, research work, science and technology. When she was finally arrested it was a scoop for counter-intelligence. They acted with patience and skill and did not pounce until they had unravelled the intricate spy ring that linked informers to dead-drops, to go-betweens and more dead-drops, and finally to Kioni, the master spy at the centre of the spy web. Twenty-eight agents and informers were arrested together with Kioni.

Switzerland, the cradle of the world banking and international affairs, is a must for Soviet Russians probing into world finance and politics. Paula Huber was a hard-working waitress in a Zürich businessmen's restaurant. She was a good waitress and very attentive to her clients' needs. Because she was dumpy and homely, her clients sensed they could call her 'Paula' with a familiarity that would not cause offence. It didn't. Paula was a sociable, comfortable woman. None of her customers, who openly discussed their financial deals and political intrigues in front of her, suspected that her small bachelor apartment concealed an ultra-modern radio-transmitter, and that twenty-seven agents and informers were working industriously to supply her with information that kept her transmitter busy. But counter-intelligence officers finally suspected it and Moscow was forced to look around to fill the gap that had abruptly appeared in its Swiss spy network.

Sofia Anatolyevna Kuzmina was trained in Prakhovka where she enrolled in the name of Gerda Schröder. After long training she was transported to Munich where she established herself as an accountant. The spy network Gerda created had long threads. She drew her information from agents in Frankfurt-am-Main, Hamburg, Stuttgart, Berlin and other important West German towns. Before the West became aware of Gerda's existence she had despatched to Moscow many pounds of microfilms and microdots.

Sometimes an unforeseen accident, rather than the skill of counter-intelligence officers, has brought about a spy's downfall. Molly O'Shea ran a dry-cleaning business in London for many years. Her espionage career came to an abrupt end when she was badly injured in a car accident. The police officers who searched her handbag for names and addresses of relatives to be summoned to her bedside had their suspicions aroused by the handbag's contents. Counter-intelligence officers were called in and the accident led to Molly's unmasking.

It was discovered that Molly had been born in Hong Kong where, at the age of forty-five, she had been recruited by the Red Chinese Secret Service. The Chinese had subjected her to blackmail pressure but when she succumbed to it they sweetened the pill with lavish rewards for her services.

Molly received a three-year course of spy training in the Canton Spy School and afterwards arrangements were made for her to travel to England and set herself up in business. The excellent use the Chinese made of Molly shows that Mao Tse-tung's Intelligence directors are more flexible than their Soviet Russian counterparts and are willing to adopt the Western method of recruiting master spies from foreigners in the target area.

Israel, which has become the home of people of many national-

ities, is probably easier to penetrate than the United Kingdom or
the United States.

Lea Hoenig had little difficulty in establishing a spy network
in Tel Aviv. She had an appropriate cover story. She was a refugee from Czechoslovakia who loved her country and was filled
with hatred for the Moscow-dominated Czech government that
had made her an exile. She was bitter because of Czechoslovakia's
total subjugation to the Kremlin's wishes and her friends tactfully avoided discussing politics in her presence, knowing her
tendency to launch into a fanatical diatribe against Russian Communism. So strong was Lea's loathing for the Communist régime
in Prague that no one suspected that for the many years she was
denouncing Russia she was simultaneously despatching to Moscow microdot information about Israel's defences, diplomacy and
economy.

Israeli counter-intelligence eventually arrested one of the many
agents in her spy web, but Moscow headquarters swiftly warned
Lea of the agent's arrest. She issued a 'May-Day' warning, so all
her agents and informers went underground. Lea, quite un-
ruffled, told her friends she was taking a long holiday. She visited
England, France and Italy, meanwhile awaiting instructions from
Moscow. For a time, Soviet Secret Service Headquarters considered sending her back to Tel Aviv, but finally decided not to take
the risk of losing her services. She was too valuable a master spy, so
she was recalled to Moscow and underwent a refresher espionage
course while awaiting a new assignment.

The refugee cover story at first seems too obvious for a spy to
adopt. But the sad truth is that in this century of moral and political conflict, there are so many refugees of all kinds, that such a
cover is quite plausible.

Marlene Kirchner was a refugee from East Germany. Like
so many Germans from the east side of the Wall she was desperate
to escape into the West German Federal Republic; like so many
East Germans, she succeeded in doing so. West Germany granted
her political asylum and in Frankfurt-am-Main she was found
employment in a hairdressing salon. She displayed great talent
for hairdressing and during the following ten months also dis-

played great talent for espionage. She built up a web of agents and informers that numbered twenty-four. But West Germany is an espionage hot-bed and counter-intelligence officers abound. Marlene's luck run out when a go-between unknowingly led spy-catchers to a dead-drop. Western spy-catchers patiently waited until Marlene walked into their trap.

Maria Fernandez was a woman spy who failed Russia miserably because of a basic unchangeable factor in her make-up; her sex!

Maria worked in Barcelona and her cover job was managing a travel bureau. It was an excellent cover, providing her with sound reason for constant contact with people travelling all over the country, and all over the world. Over many years she built up a vast spy network which extended throughout Spain and Portugal and overlapped into southern France.

The Spanish counter-intelligence service is extremely alert—vigilant not only for penetration from abroad, but for fermentation of unrest within its own borders. Nevertheless, during all the years she was operating, Maria never once came under suspicion.

But Maria had her Achilles heel. She was a woman and despite Soviet spy school conditioning and brainwashing, she could not deny her essential femininity. She fell in love with an American officer whose friendship she had cultivated with an ulterior motive, but whose masculine charm she found irresistible. Maria made her decision, abandoned her profession as master spy, married the American officer and returned with him to live in the United States.

Ceaselessly the Red women spies are weaving their webs, telling their lies and living their traitorous masquerades. Ceaselessly the counter-intelligence officers smell them out with infinite patience, hunting the big fish and neglecting the small fry. They make many arrests, but the odds are against them. It is easier to hide than to find. For every master spy who is arrested, dozens go free. For the West, and for the East, there is only one sure way to guard against the spy in your midst :

Don't talk! Careless talk costs lives!

16   Western Methods

The spy profession demands a high degree of intelligence, a quick brain, acting ability, manual skill and initiative. The woman who has these qualifications and devotes them to the service of her country must undergo training to develop her talents to the utmost. Both the West and the East realise the importance of training but they differ in their methods.

The function of a spy is to obtain information. He or she must get close to a source of information or worm into the confidence of people who have 'knowledge'. This is known as 'penetration' and a spy who penetrates deeply is known as a 'plant'. The plant is a classic form of espionage—the most historically famous example of it is the Trojan Horse.

It is upon this principle of establishing a plant that the West and East espionage methods differ most.

The Soviet Union uses a long-term system of creating plants. They select spy material from their young people, train them for long years to live like Englishmen or some other Western national and finally send them out into the field as men and women behaving, living and feeling like Western nationals.

Western espionage experts believe this is using a sledge hammer to crack a peanut. It is a painfully elaborate and time-wasting system that has a grave weakness. No matter how genuinely Western a Soviet spy may seem, it is to no avail if his or her identity documents cannot stand up to a searching examination. Very often convincing and unsuspected Soviet spies have been unmasked because of faulty documents.

Western spy trainers adopt a practical attitude. They don't manufacture plants. They concentrate upon obtaining the cooperation of people who are already plants. During the Second World War, for instance, one of Britain's most valuable spies was a woman employed in the Nazi Foreign Ministry. She had at her disposal files containing the reports received from German diplomats all over the world. The information she supplied to the Allies was of immense value. The British scored heavily simply by obtaining the cooperation of the right person in the right place.

By specialising in this form of 'penetration' the West has become skilled at obtaining the cooperation of a key person in the target area. Over and over again the West has proved this method as being more successful than the Soviet system of planning over years to plant an agent. But the Western system has its drawbacks. One big weakness is that its plant has not received the specialised espionage training that guards against detection. But Western spy instructors do not believe this is such a big handicap. An intelligent spy can swiftly learn the basic rules of self-protection. The Soviet system of long, hard years of drilling spies to be careful is unnecessary. They quote two examples to support their argument.

Agent X, a member of a British spy network in Moscow which had been operating a long time, was making a routine visit to London. His spy leader, whose code name was Nina, gave Agent X a microfilm of secret documents to take with him.

Agent X informed his Russian friends he was taking a short holiday in Britain and prepared for his departure. Soviet counter-intelligence officers are permanently stationed at Moscow Airport and are famed for their sixth sense in smelling out concealed microfilms. After some thought, Agent X decided to use his pipe as a hiding place for the microfilm.

His precautions were justified. After undergoing the usual airport formalities, he found his luggage being painstakingly searched by security officers. He waited patiently, quite unconcerned with his unlit pipe clenched between his teeth. But as the security officers' search proved unrewarding, Agent X noticed that one of them looked hard at his pipe.

Without hesitation, Agent X drew his lighter from his pocket and lit his pipe. There was a risk that if the tobacco burned down the heat and smoke would damage the microfilm. But it was a justified risk as was proved immediately.

'Just a minute,' said the security officer.

Agent X looked at him in mild surprise and puffed on his pipe. He snapped shut his lighter and returned it to his pocket.

'Let me see that lighter, please.'

Agent X smiled faintly, shrugged his shoulders and handed over the lighter.

The security officer took the lighter into a small room to examine it while Agent X puffed at his pipe placidly. He knew that the quite ordinary lighter, which could be bought over the counter of most tobacconists, was being taken apart and examined for concealed microfilms.

Nevertheless, Agent X was inwardly perturbed. He knew that Soviet watch-dogs worried a suspect like a bone when they got their teeth into him. He visualised missing the plane while he was stripped and searched.

Agent X decided to take the bull by the horns. When the security officer returned and before he could speak, Agent X said: 'What do you want now? My pipe?' He puffed smoke and then offered his pipe to the security officer. 'Go ahead. Take it apart.'

The security officer stared at the pipe impassively. 'I can see it's a very nice pipe,' he said coldly.

Agent X simmered down. 'It *is* a nice pipe, isn't it?' he said, pleased with the security officer's approval. 'Made in London. Nobody makes pipes like the British.' His pride in British workmanship seemed to make him aware how unlucky are people of other countries. He looked at his pipe, hesitated, then pretending a spontaneous gesture of generosity, again offered it to the security officer. 'You like it, you have it. It's an old friend but I'll get another in London.'

The security officer was taken by surprise.

'Take it,' urged Agent X. 'You'll never get one like it here.'

The security officer drew himself up, resenting the implication that British manufacture is better than Russian. He said coldly: 'Thank you. I don't smoke a pipe.'

As Agent X had feared, he was subjected to a thorough search.

But he did not miss his plane and throughout the search he clenched his pipe between his teeth, having allowed it to go out. To his great relief he was cleared and, soon airborne, went to the lavatory where he discovered that the protectively wrapped microfilm had survived.

Agent X had received only nine months' espionage schooling and training. His cool behaviour under such pressure is proof that the Western method of appointing agents is time-saving and effective.

Another example quoted by Western spy instructors is that of an American operator who worked for many years behind the Iron Curtain. His job was to recruit agents and informers and milk them of information. Once he had recruited an agent he severed all personal contact with him. The recruited agent passed on his information through a dead-drop. The American master spy had arranged with his agents that when they had deposited information in the dead-drop they should telephone him at an agreed time at a given number. When the operator answered, his agent merely said, 'sorry, wrong number', or some other previously arranged sentence. The master spy would thus know information was awaiting him in the dead-drop.

On one occasion, unknown to the American operator, one of his agents became suspect and was shadowed by plain-clothed state security officers. He was seen to conceal information in the dead-drop. Unaware that he was being tailed, the agent next telephoned the operator and spoke the code words agreed upon.

The following day, the operator went to collect the information from the dead-drop quite unaware that a trap had been prepared for him by the Czechoslovak counter-intelligence.

The location of the dead-drop was behind a bench in Letna Park, on a path which led out to the open countryside. It was early morning when the operator arrived to make his collection and at this time the area was usually deserted. But as the American operator strolled along the path, a presentiment of danger rang warning bells in his brain. Several men were seated on park benches reading newspapers. They were positioned so they could keep the bench in which the operator was interested under observation.

The American's step didn't falter. He strolled up to the dead-drop bench, sat down, unfolded his newspaper and began to read. He knew the other men were watching him guardedly. The American read on, idly turning the pages of his newspaper but not once glancing towards the dead-drop behind him. The other men remained stolidly seated. Presently, the American master spy yawned, folded his newspaper, rose to his feet and walked away.

Nobody followed him.

He learned later that he had walked in and out of a trap which had been laid for anyone who approached the dead-drop.

This American operator who worked successfully behind the Iron Curtain for many years without discovery, and who was so acutely alert to danger, had received only ten months' espionage schooling and training in the United States!

Sir Percy Sillitoe, K.B.E., and former head of Britain's M.I.5 has commented about the Soviet plant system that:

'It is an awful waste of time, manpower and money. I don't believe that this almost incredible method of selecting Soviet espionage recruits really safeguards Moscow against failure.'

There is also wide divergence of opinion between the West and the East about the necessity of the fanatical adherence of a spy to the political policy of his country.

The East demands blind loyalty from all its spies. It devotes years to conditioning and brainwashing its future agents to ensure their political trustworthiness. The East submits its spy students to realistic rehearsals of how they must behave if captured, and how to endure all forms of torture. Sir Percy Sillitoe has commented on this scathingly:

'This is typically Russian, and one of the heritages of Stalin's times. They are welcome to it. We, in the West, do not need this type of checking of the reliability and the breaking point of our agents; we have different ways of assessment.'

Facts are indisputable and one big indisputable fact is that there are far more Soviet agents who defect than Western agents. Despite this, Soviet espionage chiefs still insist upon elaborate training and brainwashing to ensure their spies' loyalty. Meanwhile, the West pursues the opposite policy with success.

A Soviet spy under training is not permitted to leave the institution, or to communicate with families and friends. In direct contrast, American spy cadets are granted leave passes, are unrestricted in their movement or with whom they associate and are subject to only one rigid rule : they pledge themselves not to disclose to anyone the nature of their secret training. A top-ranking American Intelligence officer has summed-up U.S. espionage training policy in these words :

'People are people and they must be treated as such. It would be very wrong to copy Russian methods and cut our students off from the outside world. Anyway, our people simply wouldn't take it. They want to live normal lives, want to go to movies, to restaurants, dances and for rides in their automobiles. And why shouldn't they? If they are content with their way of life they are more receptive to schooling and training. We don't believe in keeping our people locked up to prevent them giving away what is going on inside our establishments. Keeping them confined is no safeguard against their talking. We are dealing with intelligent people who know what they can talk about, and what they are forbidden to talk about. That sums it up, I think.'

The West uses very different raw-spy material to the East. Soviet agents begin spy training at the age of twenty after having undergone loyalty and political conditioning. The Russians hammer home repetitively every stage of a spy's training until it is indelibly impressed upon the student's mind and has become an automatic reflex reaction. The Soviet raw-spy material is conditioned like Pavlov's dogs.

An American Intelligence officer has given it as his opinion that :

'Results are far better and much more satisfactory if you educate people who are mature, and who know what they want. That's commonsense. If we use college graduates, detectives, army, navy or air force officers, teachers or people in business, or other walks of life, they have already proved themselves in a profession, and having decided to change their profession, they

are eager to learn and they consequently apply all their attention
to all they need to know in their new career.

'If we compare our method of training with the Soviet Russian
system, we find ours is the more rewarding. When training im-
mature youngsters, the Russians repeat and repeat, every single
stage of the training . . . whereas our method does not require end-
less repetition, because our people are determined to learn their
new profession and they do learn it. It is a fact that Russian training is excellent, and turns out considerable numbers of perfectly
trained master spies, but it is also a fact that Russian operators
depend more upon their training, having for most situations a
set pattern imprinted in their minds, and therefore do not so
much use their own brains as do our people. Of course, our people
are also taught the tricks of the trade, but the emphasis is not on
having for most situations a set pattern, but on individual judgment of the situation and the individual's own intelligence. Events
have proved that many more of our agents found on the spot
solutions and escaped danger, than did Russian agents.'

Apart from these important differences in methods of spy training, the East and the West follow very similar lines in espionage
tuition.

17 Western Spy Schools

All the foremost Western countries have spy schools for the training of their espionage agents. Inevitably, there are differences of opinion as to how these spy schools should be operated. An official of the French Deuxième Bureau has given his opinion:

'A really outstanding spy must be a born spy, and by "born" I mean be intelligent, quick-witted and versatile. Knowhow can be acquired from training, but what I call "the born faculty" can't. You can train any individual of reasonable intelligence to become a reasonably good spy. The Russians have some really outstanding master spies. But most of the operators who graduate from Russian spy schools are only average, equivalent to the standard of Western sub-agents. Those who became really outstanding master spies are what I call "born" spies. But the Russians will not acknowledge this human factor. They believe that top-rank master spies can be manufactured.

'I consider the Russian system of converting their nationals into fake Americans, Englishmen, Frenchmen, Germans and so on, as a lengthy and unnecessary process. We would never do this. We choose agents who are genuine citizens of their country, and our methods have achieved at least as much success behind the Iron Curtain as the Russians do in the West. Naturally, when appointing a foreign agent to work for us we take every precaution to prevent betrayal, but we cannot escape having to place our trust in a foreigner. We are willing to do this. But the Russians are not. They seldom fully trust their own people, and will almost never trust a foreigner.'

A German Secret Service director has said :

'Our schools for spies are necessary because agents must master all the techniques of intelligence work. We believe that the greatest asset of any intelligence operator is his brain—his own intelligence. While he is in the field, an agent is often faced with situations which demand his own on-the-spot decision. Success in a project, or the avoidance of detection, often depends upon our agent's personal initiative. This ability to act decisively in an emergency cannot be gained from the finest schooling or rigorous training. It is an ability which is inherent within the individual agent. The quick-witted inventiveness and judgment of our agents springs from our deliberate policy of encouraging flexibility of thought and action.'

The American and British spy schools are run on very similar lines to each other. Sir Percy Sillitoe has indicated why :

'Having only started their organised international Intelligence Service at the beginning of this century, it is only natural that the Americans drew on the age-old experiences of our Intelligence system. On the whole, their selection, schooling and training of future Intelligence agents is a very elaborate and unadulterated copy of our own system.'

All the Western countries adopt the same system of espionage. They maintain two separate organisations in foreign countries : The secret undercover spy web and the Diplomatic Intelligence Service.

The structure of the undercover spy web is common to all the Western countries. At the head of each spy web is an experienced agent who is directly responsible to Intelligence headquarters. He is known as the Resident Network Operator or the Spy Leader. All Resident Network Operators have a respectable 'cover operation' and lead a seemingly normal life in the country of their assignment. The Spy Leader is informed by Intelligence headquarters of individuals who may be approached and sounded out as possible agents and informers. He or she is provided with ample funds, which is often the most persuasive method to gain members for a spy network, but if necessary will not scruple to use blackmail. Over a period of time an efficient spy master can build up a large ring of informers and agents who provide information about military, diplomatic, economic and political developments. The master spy is the brain of the spy web and must protect himself to the utmost. It is the practice for spy masters to sever all contact with an informer or an agent once he has been recruited. Thereafter all communications are made by private codes, signals, telephone calls or dead-drops.

Inevitably, from time to time, deeply entrenched spy webs are discovered and uprooted by vigilant counter-intelligence officers. Discovery and arrest is one of the risks of the profession. But it is not long before another Resident Network Operator, who is being groomed for work in that country, is building up a new undercover spy web.

Western spy schools have their own secret methods of enrolling their students. There is undoubtedly a list of organisations from which students are drawn. Such candidates for advanced training, who may have already spent years at a university or a military college, or who have served in the police force or some other militant government corps, know they are destined to become members of the 'élite' of the Secret Service. The novice Secret Service operator has to be up to approved standards. He or she must have stamina, good health, concentration, willpower, determination and tenacity. At the spy school, sport and physical training transforms good health into toughness. Boxing, wrestling, weight-lifting, swimming, tennis and handball are on the training syllabus as is small-arms practice, shooting and unarmed combat. Western spy schools make no distinction between men and women. Women are expected to be as proficient as men in physical combat. They too study jiu-jitsu, judo, aikido and karate and become adept at rendering stronger opponents harmless or unconscious. One high-ranking instructor has said :

'It doesn't matter which of the various methods of self-defence and unarmed combat our agents master, because all of them have advantages and shortcomings. That is why we combine judo and karate. A combination of these two excellent systems equips an agent to deal with any unexpected situation which might arise. Some of our instructors are now incorporating aikido in their training and by this means we are turning out cadets who are masters in the field of unarmed combat. This specialised training is more important for women than for men. Physically, women tend to be weaker than men, but a thorough knowledge of the skills and techniques of judo, karate and aikido can balance this natural shortcoming.'

Time and again women agents in the field have had reason to be grateful for the instruction they've received in unarmed combat.

Maria was an American agent operating in Berlin. She occupied an apartment in a quiet side street and, returning home late one night, she was intercepted by two burly men.

As she was inserting her key in the front door of the block of flats where she lived, they emerged from the darkened doorway of the next building and cornered her. They said they were police officers and wished Maria to accompany them to police headquarters.

The men spoke with an accent and Maria reached a lightning decision that these men were Russian security officers. She was of slight build and once these two powerful men had her trapped in the back seat of a car, she would have no hope of resisting them if she then discovered they were not taking her to police headquarters. Quite calmly Maria made a token objection to going with them, and then reluctantly yielded to their insistence. Her manner quite persuaded the men she was convinced they were genuine police officers. But as they walked towards the waiting car, Maria galvanised into action which, for the thirty seconds it lasted, proved she was more than a match for both of them together. The man who walked half a pace in front of her she rendered unconscious with one scientific karate chop. When the second Russian agent grappled with her she used a judo throw that sent him hurtling through the air, despite his weight being double her own. The agent fell badly, and while lying on the ground half-stunned, was dealt a karate blow by Maria that silenced him too.

Maria's swift decision and determined action saved her many long years in a Soviet jail, if not her life. She learned later the two men were picked up by a West Berlin police squad car, still un-conscious. Upon interrogation at police headquarters they were proved to be Soviet Special Task officers.

West German spy schools favour aikido for unarmed combat and one of their instructors has commented :

'I consider aikido the best system. It is a little known but highly scientific series of techniques of self-defence that dates back to the Kamakura period in Japan. It was devised by a member of the Minamoto clan which was the ruling family in Japan at the time. The Minamota clan kept aikido a secret for more than two hun-dred years before it was divulged to another prominent family, the Shingan Takada. This family was equally jealous of this secret art and kept it secret for the following six hundred years, teaching it to only a few, carefully selected Japanese noblemen. It is only recently that Morihei Ueshiba, aikido's greatest living exponent, has founded his school in Tokyo and teaches this specialised art.

'Aikido is not classified as a sport. Regulated contests cannot be held—only exhibitions. Its purpose is to teach the cadet to de-fend himself in every type of hand to hand encounter. It is the perfect form of emergency self-defence and combined with karate will equip a man or woman against any attacker.'

But physical training is only a minor part of the Western spies' training. Below is a syllabus which gives an outline of the tuition which spies in Western spy schools receive.

1. GENERAL KNOWLEDGE
Comprehensive study of the world situation—political and eco-nomical.

2. SPECIALISED KNOWLEDGE
Forms of industrial organisation; conditions of industrial workers and 'peasants' in different countries; the armed forces of various countries; police; security forces; etc.

3. TACTICS
Geography, map-reading and map-drawing; codes and ciphers; communications and transmissions of information (contacts, cut-

outs, couriers, post-boxes, dead-drops); typing, shorthand, tele-printing, radio-telegraphy; photography and microfilm treat-ment; the organisation of different investigation centres abroad; relations with diplomats and other associate agents; passport and identity documents, entry and exit permits, registration of foreigners, labour permits, regulations applying to aliens abroad, diplomatic privileges; conduct in emergencies (in case of arrest, loss of documents, raids and searches and exposures by *agents provocateurs*); fieldwork; forms, range and scope of work re-quired; targets and instructions; attention to duties; psychological problems, vigilance, discretion, 'safety first', foresight, presence of mind, coolness and self-possession.

Many Western spy schools look like English public schools. Most of them are situated in country mansions surrounded by playing fields, gymnasiums, shooting ranges and laboratories. Quite frequently students are shuttled back and forth between spy schools to give them the benefit of specialised training.

As far as possible Western student-spies are prepared for field work by 'behaving' like spies. They are encouraged to make notes in their diaries, in code, but not an obvious code. They learn it is necessary to record appointments—an agent's forgetfulness has proved disastrous in the past—and how to camouflage them as genuine non-espionage appointments. Thus, if arrested, they can give a truthful explanation of the appointment entered in their diary. They learn to assume all telephone lines are tapped and all telephone conversations are conducted in double-talk. The double-talk must be a verbal code that seems to be normal con-versation to any monitor. Agents learn that private apartments, hotel rooms, even if behind locked doors, are not the safest meet-ing places. They are encouraged to use public places, a crowded street corner, a railway station or a cinema foyer for a rendezvous. A good agent lives with the conviction he or she is being constantly shadowed and behaves accordingly. Upon arrival in a town the agent never goes straight to his rendezvous. He or she drifts there by a devious route, changing the form of transport several times, wandering through crowded stores and out by a different door.

When there is more than one rendezvous on the same day, the agent habitually makes appointments at widely separated points. And he or she will never under any circumstances go direct from one rendezvous to another. The importance of punctuality is stressed. No agent will wait for more than one or two minutes at a rendezvous. Anyone who loiters can arouse suspicion.

During the student-spy's training an instructor may ask at any time for a handbag or pockets to be turned out. The student is then expected to give a satisfactory explanation of every item, as though police interest has been aroused after the student had been involved in an accident or an arrest. The student-spy learns that, tiresome as it may be, it is essential to take a thousand seemingly unnecessary precautions rather than arouse any suspicion. The price an agent is called upon to pay for one small failure is high.

The Western spy school training seldom exceeds a year. But it is a highly concentrated course and quite a few emerge from it qualified to go into the field. But those who have the natural 'born' ability to qualify after such a short training prove themselves to be more capable than their Russian counterparts who have to be 'conditioned' for many years.

18   The Tools of the Trade

Scientific aids to spying are such an integral part of espionage that experts continuously invent and construct new and ingenious devices to help agents in the field.

CAMERAS

A spy can often gain access to important documents for a short time, but dare not remove them without exposing himself to arrest. The camera is the spy's best answer when he or she is faced with this problem. But the mere possession of a camera is liable to arouse suspicion; the scientific brains of the West and the East have, therefore, concentrated upon producing ever smaller cameras.

Considerable success has been achieved. In regular use now are wristwatches which do not merely tell the time. They are also miniature cameras, made with such skill and precision that accurate microfilms can be taken under bad lighting conditions. Not only do these miniature cameras efficiently perform the work of a much larger camera, they are also so skilfully camouflaged that only an experienced security officer is able to detect that the watch serves a dual purpose.

What has been done with watches is done with other everyday articles the average man or woman carries with him. The Americans have perfected a microfilm spy camera concealed within a fountain pen. The pen can be used for writing yet the concealed camera contains enough film to photograph a considerable number of documents. Reloading casettes are supplied to the spy and the camera can be instantly reloaded in bright daylight. Cigarette lighters are often used to house miniature cameras. The lighter's butane gas capacity is reduced, giving only three or four days' use before recharging. But when the gas-filling screw is removed the lens concealed behind it is ready for action. Cigarette case cameras are now going out of fashion; by modern standards they are too clumsy and too commonplace, although they have advantages over their ultra-miniature successors. The cigarette case camera is fully automatic and large documents or blueprints can be copied by holding the cigarette case against the document and running it up and down the page while the microfilm inside unreels automatically, taking dozens of photographs. Later, when the microfilm is developed and enlarged and pieced together, a perfect reproduction of the original document is obtained.

Microfilm cameras are concealed inside hearing aids, in pocket transistors, in ladies' compacts, spectacle cases and clothes brushes. Almost any everyday article in the possession of a spy may be the home for a cunningly concealed microfilm camera.

TELEVISION

Science has not neglected television as an aid to spying. Transistorised television cameras, operated by hearing-aid batteries and as small as a lady's handbag, are manufactured by espionage scientists. Their small size permits them to be hidden easily; behind books on a shelf, taped to the underside of a table or with underclothing in a drawer. These TV cameras are equipped with an ingenious 'seeing' eye that consists of a thin, flexible rod which can be thrust under the door of a locked room, through a keyhole or through a small hole knocked in the wall. This flexible rod can bend light and can televise images around right-angled corners. Such cameras are not in common use but at times are of immense value to a spy.

Sometimes agents must maintain a continuous watch on a building. During daylight this can be done with a carefully focused television camera, but when night falls the ordinary television camera is useless. Scientists have overcome this problem by developing transistorised devices, with pick-ups, which convert the infra-red heat-waves emitted by human beings and other objects into visible light. By the use of this infra-red invention, a darkened building can be kept under observation at a distance of five hundred feet and individuals can be identified in the dark at a distance of more than a hundred feet.

MICROPHONES

But visual spying is rarely essential and 'eavesdropping' is much simpler, less dangerous and almost as effective. Scientists have excelled themselves in the manufacture of miniature microphones.

'Limpet' microphones have been widely and successfully used since the mid-fifties. A limpet attached to the outside of a building can pick up every word and sound within the room nearest to it. The most commonly used limpet is smaller than a matchbox. They receive and transmit by ultra-short-wave radio to a radius of five miles. Knowing that a conference is to take place within a certain well-guarded area, a secret agent need only attach a limpet to the outside wall of the building where the conference is to take place, and thereafter can sit in a car, or a hotel room anything up to five miles away, watching a tape-recorder register every word spoken at the secret conference. This recording can then be played over, its contents typed out, reduced to microdot size and soon be on its way to Secret Service headquarters.

The first officially acknowledged discovery of a limpet was one announced by the Iranian Embassy in Moscow. This limpet was attached outside the Ambassador's first-floor office probably by a window cleaner. Between 1956 and 1965, limpets were constantly being found on the outside of Allied buildings in West Berlin and various centres of the West German Federal Republic, in Paris, Belgium, London, Washington, Rome and in many other countries of the free world. Both the American and British Embassies in Moscow were constantly locating electronic listening devices, while Soviet Russia and other satellite countries found similar spy listening devices in the Soviet Secret Service headquarters, the Foreign Ministry and other administrative buildings in Moscow as well as in Budapest, Leipzig, Prague and Warsaw.

But the West lagged behind in the exploitation of electronic ears. In the spring of 1964 Security officers at the U.S. Embassy in Moscow knew there must be a security leak somewhere *inside* the Embassy. Just once again another careful, painstaking search of the premises was conducted. It yielded no results. But then a Security officer recalled that *before* the Embassy was moved into Tschaikovsky Street in 1953, the building that now housed the American Embassy had then been seven stories high. In preparation for the American occupation, Soviet workmen had added another three stories. Once again the Security officers searched, this time breaking away plaster and brickwork. American faces turned red. The thick interior walls of the three top stories of the American Embassy contained a network of wires connecting up forty microphones! Each microphone was attached to a wooden peg that extended through the thick walls almost to the surface of the plaster. For more than a decade the hundreds of conferences held in the U.S. Embassy had been transmitted direct to Soviet Intelligence headquarters!

Less than a year later, in May 1965, the United States despatched nine Navy Seabees to Warsaw to undertake the debugging of its Embassy. A few weeks later the State Department requested Congress to approve a grant of $1,644,600 for the purpose of debugging other United States Embassies.

Yet, twenty years earlier, in 1945, the Russians had demonstrated to the Americans that they should tread warily. Soviet diplomats in Moscow, with bland friendliness, presented Mr. W. Averell Harriman, the then United States Ambassador to the Soviet Union, a carved replica of the United States Great Seal. Mr Harriman was touched by this Russian gesture of goodwill. He proudly accorded this replica the place of honour in his own Ambassadorial study, in the U.S. Embassy.

It wasn't until 1952 that American Security officers discovered the shield was an ingenious spying device. It was made of wood and within its thickness was a hollowed-out cavity. Inside the cavity was a U-shaped piece of metal to which was attached a steel spring vibrator. This delicate steel spring vibrated to the sound-waves of conversations held in the Ambassador's study. Directly across the street from the Embassy, Soviet Intelligence agents had installed a highly sensitive continuous-wave radar device which was focused upon the steel spring vibrator. The radar receiver was so sensitive it could register the vibrations produced by human speech and convert them into intelligible sound! For seven years every word spoken in the Ambassador's office was monitored by the Russians.

The discovery of this Russian trick put U.S. Security officers on the track of other ingenious Soviet listening devices. They learned the Russians had developed a method of recording conversations in a room by tuning in to the vibration of the window pane. A beam of ultrasonic energy was focused on the window pane and a sonar tube device converted its vibrations into intelligible speech. Even better, when they could Soviet Intelligence officers replaced the glass of an ordinary window pane with a pane made of electrically conductive glass.[1] A highly sensitive continuous-wave radar beam focused upon such a window pane can easily convert the vibrations into speech.

Western agents long ago learned that any window protected by the conventional metal-foil strip used as a burglar alarm is a gift for spies. The vibrations of the metal foil can be captured by radar at a considerable distance.

Western scientists who have been concentrating upon reducing the size of spying devices have achieved sensational results. They have perfected a listening device measuring little more than a quarter of an inch in diameter but so selective that, although concealed in a hollowed-out table leg or in upholstered furniture, it can pick up any sound in the room. This device has one drawback, however, in that its transmitting range is limited to a quarter of a mile. But this drawback can be easily overcome. Once the listening device is planted in a building, a miniature wire recorder, only a fraction larger than a 'hidden ear', is concealed in the same building in an easily accessible hiding place, where the recording cassettes can be easily renewed.

TRANSMITTERS

American scientists have manufactured a radio transmitter no larger than a small lump of sugar. It is a frequency-modulated

[1] This is leaded glass treated with a transparent film of tin oxide.

transmitter, using one to five transistors which can transmit for several miles and broadcast nonstop for a hundred hours on the power of its tiny battery. When concealed in a car battery or a telephone it can draw its power from the car battery or the telephone system.

American agents sometimes turn themselves into walking radio transmitters. They wear a neck-cord antenna under their shirt or blouse and the transmitter is so small it usually escapes detection even if the agent is frisked by security officers. It is believed by some theoreticians that such a device was used in the assassination of President Kennedy. They argue that a number of marksmen were aiming rifles at the President, and in order to ensure a simultaneous volley of shots, each gunman was to press his trigger on the count of five. An observer close to President Kennedy's car was to count slowly as it neared the selected site of execution. But . . . how could he communicate with the scattered marksmen? It is said that the gunmen were equipped with small receivers and that the fatal counting was pronounced by a man who stood close to the convoy as it approached. He raised his umbrella in the air for a few seconds and had a miniature transmitter close to his mouth. His upraised umbrella concealed the antenna.

Now that scientists have solved the problem of manufacturing miniature transmitters their use is limited only by the imagination of their owner. They can be hung from their own twelve-inch antennae in the folds of window curtains, beneath a skirt or under trousers. They can be concealed and connected to waterpipes and railings, or even a metal bedstead when the transmission range is greatly increased by the use of this metal antenna. A miniature transmitter, concealed in a handbag 'carelessly' left in an office and retrieved later, can record all that has ensued in the owner's absence.

TELEPHONE INTERCEPTORS

Western bugging is now so skilful that Soviet Russia and her satellite countries never permit outside workmen to install telephones, repair electrical faults or renew the plumbing in their Embassies. They employ only their own carefully screened technicians and electricians who are provided with diplomatic passports and status. One satellite country, suspecting its Embassy was 'bugged', brought in an army of workmen to carry out a complete overhaul. These 'diplomats' spent weeks digging a trench several feet deep in the grounds that surrounded the Embassy, vainly searching for buried wires.

Telephones must always be suspect; miniature interceptors can be attached almost anywhere along a telephone line. To ensure that telephone conversations are not monitored the entire telephone line would need to be bared and examined every day. This is impractical. The only safe way to deal with telephone interceptors is to avoid discussing secret matters on the telephone.

INFRA-RED BEAMS

There are ingenious and intricate listening devices. A portable laser microphone exists which emits an invisible infra-red beam that will pass through a window pane and bounce off a miniature mirrored modulator concealed in a convenient place. The deflected beam is captured many miles away by a photo amplifier which decodes every word spoken in the room where the modulator is concealed.

Even an electronic listening device has been produced that is camouflaged as a car spotlight. Cunningly concealed within the spotlight is a Doppler radar microphone connected to the car's radio. The car can be parked miles away from a house under observation so long as it has a clear view of the building. A narrow-band signal is bounced off the window pane by speech vibrations, and an agent can sit in his car and listen to the conversation on the car's radio.

'INVISIBLE' INK

A hundred years ago the exchange of secret messages was aided by 'invisible' ink. The materials used were primitive. One method was to write a letter in ordinary ink, leaving wide margins and spaces between the lines. The secret message was written in the margins and between the lines of handwriting in ordinary milk. If the paper was of the right colour, the secret message was not easily visible once the milk had dried. Upon receipt of the letter, the spy recipient had only to scorch the letter before a fire and the words written in milk would turn brown.

But such outdated invisible ink methods cannot apply in the late twentieth century. Or can they?

An American agent who has worked for years in a Russian town has regularly communicated with her U.S. Central Intelligence Agency superiors using invisible ink. But there is no comparison between modern invisible ink and the invisible inks used a generation ago. Scientists, using microscopes which can break down the atomic structure of liquids, have perfected invisible inks which can defy detection.

The procedure adopted by the modern spy is to write out a message with the invisible ink on an ordinary plain piece of paper. As long as the invisible ink remains wet it is discernible and the message can be checked over. The ink takes a few minutes to dry and is then completely invisible, even when examined under a powerful microscope. At least an hour must elapse before the spy can write or type an apparently harmless message over the invisible writing. He or she takes care to avoid suspicion by not leaving wide margins or wide spaces between the lines. Even if the letter is intercepted and submitted to chemical tests, it is unlikely the use of invisible ink will be detected. When it arrives at its destination and is chemically treated, the invisible ink message emerges in such a deep black it is easily readable through ordinary ink or typewritten lettering of a lighter colour.

The American agent who used this system so long and so successfully said:

'Having examined every letter I received during my first two years in the town, I knew they were being opened. So was most of the mail I sent to my superiors via "cover" addresses. My communications, written in invisible ink, were never discovered. If they had been, I would have been unable to continue my activities. In any case, if the invisible ink had been discovered while on its way to its recipient, my secret messages would have been made visible. Once this has happened, there is no way to render them invisible again. All my communications were received safely and in none of them had the invisible ink been developed and made legible.'

This agent, who lived dangerously for so many years, knew her apartment was being periodically searched. She took certain measures, so that she knew every time her apartment had been subjected to another secret search. The invisible ink was kept in a toilet bottle. The top section of the bottle contained scented hair lotion, the bottom section housed the invisible ink. The processing liquid for making invisible ink messages visible she concealed in another ingenious way but she did not divulge the details.

A French agent working in Warsaw, who has successfully evaded suspicion for many years, said :

'Microdot and microfilm communications play the most important role. But having a secondary means of communication is of tremendous value. Microfilms are essential for transmitting blueprints, documents, etc. But personal reports and certain other information do not need to be microfilmed or microdotted and then invisible ink serves its purpose.'

DRUGS

Tasteless and fast-acting drugs are an essential part of spy's equipment and can often be utilised to great advantage. Rita Elliott, Russia's master spy in Australia, used a specially manufactured drug very successfully. Western agents too have made good use of fast-acting drugs.

A French Secret Service officer has said :

'Although international records prove some agents succeed in drugging their victims with specially prepared chocolates or other edibles, or by dropping dope in their drinks, this method depends very much on chance, and upon the alertness of the victims. In my view, which is shared by most Intelligence experts, the best method to drug anybody is as follows : Having ascertained the victim is not a teetotaller I lace *every* bottle in my cocktail cabinet with the drug I wish to use. Even the most cautious person has his suspicions lulled when he picks his drink from a wide range of bottles, sees his host pour the same drink from the same bottle into his own glass, and then be the first to drink it. Normally this would result in two people being drugged instead of the victim only. But I take the precaution of rendering myself immune to the drugged drink with an antidote before the victim arrives. In this way, success is virtually a certainty. All you need is the right drug, and the right antidote.'

Some of a spy's drugs are deadly. They are carried in small phials or are made up into pills. Unless the agent has a very special mission, such deadly drugs are intended only to meet a dire emergency. If a spy is arrested and subjected to extreme torture he may choose to use this means to avoid suffering or giving away vital secrets. There are a number of officially recorded cases of Allied and German spies adopting these extreme measures during the Second World War. Many of the Nazi war leaders, including Hermann Göring, preferred suicide to being tried and executed by their captors. Francis Gary Powers, the American U-2 pilot-spy, was in possession of a fast-acting poison when his aircraft was brought down over Russian territory. If Powers had thought it necessary, he too could have avoided arrest and interrogation; but Powers decided to live.

Specialised training and mechanical aids are available in abundance to help the master spy and his sub-agents. But over and over again it has been proved that the telling factor in the success of espionage is the human element.

Spies constantly find themselves faced with situations which cannot be covered by training, textbooks or recorded experiences. It is then that the quick thinking, sometimes reckless initiative of the spy involved can save a mission from failure.

Such initiative was demonstrated by a woman Resident Network Operator working in Prague on behalf of the U.S. Intelligence. By various methods this woman spy had come into possession of a microfilm of important blueprints. There was no difficulty about despatching the microfilm to headquarters. But, additionally, she had come into possession of an actual 'part' of what was believed to be a revolutionary innovation in guided missiles. The master spy knew this part could be invaluable to American scientists and technologists.

How could she smuggle it to Washington? She learned that a Czechoslovak government car was leaving for Munich. She decided to conceal the small 'part' in this official car. But how?

The car was being overhauled in a government garage workshop and was scheduled to leave within twenty-four hours. The master spy had a contact who was employed in the office of the government workshop. Several attempts were made by this contact to get into the garage, but each time she was frustrated. The last time, the contact (who had concealed the part not too successfully in the bodice of her dress) came close to discovery when Secret Police Security guards initiated a snap search of individuals inside the workshop just as she arrived upon the threshold. She turned and walked back to the office, having been only seconds away from arrest. Every precaution was being taken to safeguard the lives of the high-ranking government officials who would be travelling in the car.

The master spy became agitated as the hours passed and she came no closer to achieving her objective. Then luck smiled upon her. Her contact reported that the rear seat of the car had been found to be damaged; the entire back seat was being removed so it could be re-upholstered. Upholstery was an outside job and the seat was sent to another workshop.

There was less security supervision in this upholstery workshop and by using another agent, the master spy was able to have the guided missile part concealed in the back seat. Later, when the official car arrived in Munich, U.S. agents were waiting and ready to recover the valuable piece of evidence.

This vital part would never have reached the West if the initiative of the woman master spy had been disciplined out of her by long years of training to work by rule of thumb.

19   'Operation Anne'

One of the most amazing British women spies is officially recorded simply as 'Anne'.

The Second World War was going badly for Britain when one of its Intelligence chiefs was brought a sealed letter by his secretary. It was a personal recommendation from a trusted friend asking him to interview the person subsequently given the code name of Anne in British Intelligence secret records.

'She is waiting outside,' said the secretary.

The Intelligence chief read the letter of recommendation again. Anne was in her thirties and had given her services to ambulance, rescue and civil defence work. She had given it up some weeks earlier on doctor's orders.

'Show her in,' sighed the Intelligence officer. He knew already he could make no use of the woman.

Anne was a small, frail-looking woman who perched nervously on the edge of the visitor's chair and looked at him across the desk with big, thoughtful eyes.

'I understand you wish to work for this department?'

Anne nodded eagerly. 'I must help defeat those beastly Nazis,' she said with feeling. She smiled wryly. 'I drove an ambulance for a time but my health let me down.'

The Intelligence officer nodded. 'What do you think you could do for us?' he asked gently.

'I can get you information from the enemy.'

'That would be useful,' said the Intelligence officer. 'But it's not easy, especially for somebody in ill-health. For our work, a high standard of physical health is necessary.'

'I wouldn't exert myself,' said Anne simply. Her eyes looked even bigger and childlike. 'I can just sit here and get you information.'

The Intelligence officer was a busy man; he mentally classified Anne as a 'nut', but her letter of recommendation restrained him from bringing the interview to an abrupt end. He asked gently : 'How can you obtain information about the enemy while sitting in that chair?'

Anne answered patiently : 'I possess the gift of being able to leave my body and roam at will.'

'Indeed?'

'You don't believe me,' smiled Anne. 'Nobody does. But don't worry. I'm quite used to people thinking I'm crazy.'

'You *have* made a rather unusual statement,' agreed the Intelligence officer tactfully.

'I can prove what I say.' Anne eyed him speculatively. 'Will you give me the opportunity?'

The Intelligence officer decided the best way to get rid of Anne was to allow her to prove that her claims were nonsense. 'Very well.'

Anne drew her chair closer to the desk, sat up straight and talked crisply : 'I will remain in the room with you. You will instruct somebody in the building to conduct a conversation with any person he chooses. He is to start this conversation when you tell him, and is to record it. I will leave my body, which will remain here, and listen to the conversation. When I return I will tell you everything I have heard.'

The Intelligence officer stared at her hard. Then he reached for his telephone.

'Are you ready?'

'I need a few minutes to compose myself.'

The Intelligence officer spoke to a subordinate and ordered him to begin a conversation with a colleague in five minutes. He hung up.

Anne sat back in the deep leather armchair, closed her eyes and presently began to breathe deeply. The Intelligence officer watched her warily, suspicious of trickery. Quite soon Anne seemed to fall asleep. After a time her eyelids fluttered, she shivered and then sat up. Abruptly she was wide awake.

'It was boring,' she said.

'Yes?'

'I travelled to the room where your officers were talking,' Anne informed him. She then told him the names of the officers and said they had looked at a copy of *The Times* and concentrated their attention upon the adverts. She repeated their conversation and added that each advert they'd talked about they'd encircled with blue pencil.

The Intelligence officer telephoned his subordinate. To his utter astonishment everything Anne had told him was confirmed by the young officers.

He replaced the telephone and looked at Anne with new respect. 'Is your mind-travelling limited?'

'I can go *anywhere*.'

'You do understand you will have to submit yourself to other much more stringent tests?'

'I would prefer it,' said Anne confidently. 'I want you to be convinced.'

During the following days and weeks Anne underwent many carefully prepared tests which even involved her reporting conversations between British officers serving overseas. To every test she gave such startlingly accurate reports that the hard-headed British Intelligence officers were finally convinced Anne could 'mind-travel'.

Anne was submitted to a final test. She was an educated woman who had spent many months as a student in Berlin and Zürich before the war, and had a good working knowledge of German. Her final test took Anne to Nazi headquarters in Berlin! Her report upon this act of 'mind-travel' could not be immediately checked, but everything she said was recorded. At Nazi headquarters she had picked up a certain amount of information about military movements. Within the next few days these same military manœuvres were put into action by the Germans. British Intelligence decided to enrol Anne on the staff.

'It's a pity you cannot bring back documents when you "mind-

E

travel'',' sighed a British Intelligence officer.

'It is not necessary,' said Anne. 'I have a photographic memory. When I wish, I can stare at a document intently until it becomes imprinted upon my mind. Later, I can read it off as though I'm holding the document in my hand.'

Anne was sent on many 'mind-travelling' expeditions. Any information she brought back to British Secret Service headquarters was treated as respectfully as information provided by other spies. British political and military strategy was influenced and helped by Anne's reports.

In common with other British Secret Service agents, Anne's true identity must remain secret. Her help to her country and her very special 'talents' have never been acknowledged publicly. This is as Anne has wished. She is by nature a shy and retiring person.

Nevertheless, having been told about Operation Anne by one of her war-time superior Intelligence officers, I was, by a round-about means, able to trace Anne and meet her unofficially.

She is a gentle, elderly lady living quietly and gracefully in retirement. She devotes a certain amount of time to Spiritualism. She is a trance-medium and is happy to be able to give a measure of consolation to bereaved people wanting to contact loved ones who have passed over.

Anne still possesses the gift of 'mind-travel'. But she rarely practises it these days. It is a gift she uses with great discretion. She would not wish to eavesdrop, or intrude into people's private lives. Regretfully, her rare gift is one which is difficult to put to good use.

It was only during the war, when the bestiality of the Nazis threatened to destroy every good humane instinct, that Anne felt she could use her gift to a great purpose.

I persuaded Anne to give me proof she could still 'mind-travel'. She was reluctant to do so without having good reason. But I was very insistent and she gave me an astonishing demonstration of her ability to report correctly events occurring far away from her physical sight and hearing.

I tried to persuade Anne to tell me about some of her most important spying assignments for British Intelligence during the last war. She flatly refused. She has sworn to the Official Secrets Act and Anne is a woman of integrity. Anne's spying assignments during the war will never be recounted by her.

20 Natasha

Most Intelligence headquarters have vast offices devoted to filing the dossiers of their own and 'foreign' spies. One of the most interesting records is the case history of an American woman spy operating in the Soviet Union, because it provides overwhelming proof of the success of the Western system of recruiting spies in the target area behind the Iron Curtain.

Natasha was a Russian civil servant employed at the heart of Moscow's administration. She was ideally situated for espionage and for this reason was approached by American Intelligence officers.

It cannot be revealed how Natasha was persuaded to become a Western spy. Blackmail may have been used or money may have proved tempting. There could have been other, more subtle methods of persuasion—the West has grown practised at converting Russians and other Iron Curtain nationals to be willing cooperators with the West.

Natasha pleasantly surprised her new superiors. When, with some difficulty since it all took place in Moscow, Natasha was given a few months' special training in Western espionage methods, she proved herself to be so efficient and eager to aid the West that her superiors decided to employ her as a master spy, instead of as a sub-agent. It was a wise and sound decision. Natasha knew her own people as no foreigner could ever know them. She recruited agents and informers with great foresight and within eight months of becoming a master spy, she had a perfectly functioning spy ring established in all of the Kremlin's administrative offices. By exercising shrewd judgment and selecting the right person in the target area, American Intelligence gained a spy network that penetrated the very walls of the Kremlin!

Natasha obeyed the rules prescribed for the protection of a resident spy. Once she had selected and recruited an agent, she severed all contact thereafter with that person. She devised her own system of go-betweens and dead-drops which were so ingenious she was never suspected, nor interrogated. She operated with such cool audacity she even used the library inside the Kremlin as a dead-drop. Some of her agents and informers passed on microfilms by concealing them in books they had borrowed. When the books were returned to the library, the go-between librarian recommended the same books to other sub-agents for reading. The sub-agents borrowed the books, removed the microfilms in the secrecy of their homes, and conveyed them to the next dead-drop.

It is astonishing but true that Natasha's spy network, which operated efficiently for so many years, comprised dozens of spies who had received only the minimum espionage training under the greatest difficulties. The Russians, who give all spies a minimum of ten years' training, would regard them as rank amateurs. Nevertheless, they operated within the very heart of the Kremlin and none was ever arrested.

Natasha's flow of vital information to Washington was rated high and her requests were given 'first-class priority'. At her suggestion U.S. experts manufactured a miniature hair-wire recorder that could be concealed within a woman's walking shoe. All the scientific ingenuity of the West was concentrated for many weeks on this project, after which three of Natasha's agents attended important top-level conferences and recorded every word spoken. These battery hair-wire recorders operated many hours non-stop and the shoes were designed so that the recording cartridges could be changed within seconds. Kremlin Security officers always search secret conference rooms with a fine toothcomb, hoping to discover bugging devices, before any conference is convened. They can always assure their superiors with utmost confidence that the conference room is 'clean'. But Natasha's agents who attended the conferences could always provide Washington with a full transcript of the secret proceedings.

Natasha's long service to the U.S. Intelligence Service could not have been accomplished if she had not followed the strict security rules, remained completely detached from her informers and agents and never attempted to obtain secret information herself. She disobeyed this last rule on only one special occasion. A Soviet-trained spy, brainwashed and conditioned, will *never* disobey rules, but Natasha used her initiative and acted decisively. She was later severely reprimanded by her superiors for exposing herself to danger, but it was conceded that in view of *all* the circumstances, she had probably made the right decision.

She had found herself, because of her job, within the confines of a closely guarded scientific-technological 'top grade' department. While she performed routine work for her superior whom she accompanied, she knew that within easy reach were secret files containing blueprints of important experimental work. These blueprints were on loan to the department, had been studied carefully and were due to be returned that same afternoon. Microfilms of these blueprints would be of immense value to Washington. It was not Natasha's job to collect information, but she was a master spy and this was a unique opportunity. If she could microfilm those blueprints she could save the United States millions of dollars and thousands of scientific workmen-hours. She made her decision. If it was at all possible, whatever the risks, she would microfilm these blueprints!

It seemed that the opportunity to do so was handed to her on a plate. Her superior and his colleague decided to tour the workshop. This meant she was left alone in the office. However, as soon as her superior left a security guard entered the office and engaged Natasha in conversation. He was a pleasant, friendly young man but alert and trained to be suspicious of everybody. Natasha had no doubt the guard's orders were to keep the office under surveillance during his superior's absence.

Natasha chatted with the security officer and a warm companionship sprang up between them. The precious minutes ticked past. Presently there was a knock on the door, it opened and Natasha saw a rubber-tyred trolley bearing a steaming Samovar.[1]

[1] A Russian tea-urn.

'Tea for two,' announced the security officer.

This was when the master spy made the decision to gamble desperately.

Her calm face concealed her inner excitement as she stirred sugar into her tea. She distracted the security officer's attention for a few moments and risked shaking a few drops of colourless liquid into his tea. Her friendliness had lulled any suspicion the security officer might have had and he failed to notice her quick movement. Within minutes of drinking his tea he slumped in his chair, efficiently drugged.

Natasha worked swiftly. At any moment her superior might open the door. But she took the risk. She microfilmed all the blueprints classified as 'top secret'. But when the filming was finished she was still in danger. She removed the microfilm roll from the camera, taped it to the underside of the desk, and also found a suitable safe hiding place for the camera; the film and camera could be retrieved later by another of her agents who worked in the building. She checked she had not overlooked anything that could betray her.

Her biggest problem was the security officer. She could not conceal that he had been drugged. She shook two more colourless drops into her own half-drunk tea and, having disposed of the drug container where it would not be found, braced herself and drank her tea.

Ten minutes later, when her superiors returned, they found Natasha and the security officer in a drugged stupor.

Doctors, security guards and laboratory workers were summoned instantly. Natasha and the security officer were aroused but neither remembered anything except feeling sleepy after drinking tea. The dregs in the tea-cups were analysed and found to contain an instantly acting sleeping drug.

For two long days security guards vigorously interrogated all the staff in the building while special security agents checked all the classified top secret documents in the files. None were missing. It was finally concluded an abortive attempt had been made to drug the security guard, and Natasha who happened to be with him had accidentally been drugged at the same time.

Strict security measures were introduced to guard against any future drugging.

Some days later, one of Natasha's agents, who worked in the building, invented a justifiable excuse for visiting the office. She found the microfilm still taped to the underside of the desk, recovered the camera from its hiding place and conveyed both to a prepared dead-drop in another part of the building. Soon, through the chain of dead-drops and go-betweens the microfilm was once again in Natasha's hands. Two weeks later the top secret blueprints were being examined by American technicians.

Natasha's gamble met with success and the value of the documents she microfilmed justified the risk. But she was ordered never to take a similar risk again. For a few desperate minutes she had jeopardised not only her own freedom but the security of an entire spy network. Despite the immense value of the microfilmed blueprints, Natasha had been imprudent and merited a severe reprimand.

The unmasking of a master spy can lead to immense dangers for her superiors. Clever counter-intelligence officers can sometimes take over an entire spy network from a master spy and operate it themselves, skilfully feeding the master spy's superiors with false information that can affect their diplomatic and military strategy disastrously.

Natasha was never arrested, nor were any members of her spy ring ever captured. But Moscow's Secret Service files show that their Intelligence officers became aware that a master spy was operating within the Kremlin. Those same secret files fail to state why the master spy ceased to operate within the Kremlin; nor do they reveal any knowledge of the spy's identity.

Why Natasha ceased to be a master spy, and what happened to her afterwards, are questions only the U.S. Secret Service can answer. But Washington is keeping this information strictly secret. Yet it can be safely assumed that Natasha is continuing her valuable work for the United States in the Soviet Union.

21 Wanda

Antek was a laboratory assistant working in one of Poland's most important secret research establishments. He was an intelligent but rather brash young man with a tendency to drink too much and spend too freely. Some years previously—because he'd proposed at his local Communist Party branch an idea to which he stubbornly clung, but which was vetoed by his comrades—he had earned the reputation within the party of being a political waverer. He resented this accusation, considered it was malicious and unjustified, and believed promotion had been withheld from him at his place of work because of this. His spendthrift nature made him dissatisfied with his earnings, which he thought should have been much more and he nursed a grievance against the Communist Party that had deprived him of a more influential post. Nevertheless, his girlfriend Olga, with whom he one day hoped to set up house, was a fine companion and help-mate, and he could always let off steam about his grievances by confiding them to her. It was reassuring to know that he could grumble and complain bitterly about the Communist Party to Olga without his confidences being betrayed.

However, there were others who also knew of Antek's grievances and one day he was approached by a French Secret Service agent who not merely sympathised with the Pole's grumbles but indicated how he might augment his slender income with satisfyingly generous bonuses. Antek snapped at the bait, and after preliminary training was rated as a qualified espionage agent. His task was to microfilm important research reports and deposit them in a dead-drop.

Antek now found life much more enjoyable. But despite the stern warnings given by his French employers, his spendthrift nature asserted itself. Unobtrusively he spent more money than he earned.

Spending more than one's income is always a sign of shiftlessness even in Western countries. Tax evaders, confidence tricksters and criminals often draw unwanted attention to themselves by spending money they cannot prove they possess lawfully. In Communist-controlled Poland, which swarms with private Security Police, even unobtrusive over-spending becomes conspicuous.

Antek soon came under suspicion and was tailed by State Security agents. A Secret Police officer made friends with Antek in a bar one evening, bought him drinks and encouraged him to talk. Antek drank so much his tongue ran away with him. Completely intoxicated he boasted he knew a way to make a fortune by microfilming secret research reports!

Antek sobered up quickly when he was immersed in a bath of ice-cold water at interrogation headquarters. But by that time even clear headedness could serve him little. He had already talked too much and was subjected to the long and painful process of telling everything he knew.

Yet, once again the proved and trusted structure of a spy network stood firm against penetration by spy catchers.

Antek told everything he knew. But the *only* thing he knew was the dead-drop where he deposited his microfilms and where payment awaited him. Antek's interrogators were unable to extract from him the names of any other members of the spy network for the simple reason that he did not know them.

But once the Secret Police knew the location of Antek's dead-drop, by keeping it under constant surveillance they could probably trap another agent or go-between. Orders were issued for security officers to keep non-stop watch over the dead-drop. It seemed that by a slow process of trapping agents at dead-drops, interrogation and torture, the entire spy network might be rolled up.

Antek's name disappeared from all the official records a few weeks later. It is not known what was the verdict of the judges at

the secret trial which he may have attended. He may have been
sentenced to death, or to life imprisonment.

Antek had not revealed to any of his friends that he had been
recruited as a spy and his girlfriend, Olga, was the last person
he would have weighed down with such a guilty secret. It would
have placed upon her the onus of reporting him to the authorities,
or also becoming a traitor to her country. Antek's affection for
Olga was too strong for him to expose her to such a risk.

So Antek was quite unaware that Olga was an agent in the
very same spy ring! It had been Olga who, listening to Antek's
bitter complaints about the Communist Party, had passed on the
recommendation that Antek might be suitable material for recruiting into the French espionage network. She'd made her suggestion to Wanda who was her sister and also the spy web's master
spy in Warsaw.

Antek had been due to meet Olga later on the same night he
was arrested. When he'd failed to keep the appointment Olga
made cautious enquiries and learned Antek was in custody and
his room had been ransacked by the Secret Police. She warned
Wanda who sent out a May-Day signal to all agents and informers, sending them underground and prohibiting them from using
any dead-drop for passing on microfilms or communicating with
her in any other way.

Using the coded system of communications that Antek had
revealed to them, the Secret Police sent out a signal that important
information was waiting in Antek's dead-drop. But Wanda knew
the code-call was a trap, because sources open to her had confirmed that Antek's dead-drop was under surveillance by Secret
Police agents. So once more the espionage rule which states that
agents and informers shall never meet the master spy had proved
an invaluable safety measure.

Wanda was employed by the Polish Airline LOT. She had
been recruited into the French Secret Service in the spring of
1961 while employed in the Paris branch office of the airline. She
was intelligent and efficient and by Christmas 1961, after having

been sent back to Poland, she began building up her spy network. Her second-in-command was her sister, Olga, the girlfriend of the ill-fated Antek.

Wanda occupied an influential position in LOT and her close contact with airline personnel enabled her to use a unique method for speedy delivery service of microfilms and other important espionage material to her superiors. It can now be revealed that she had a simple but effective means of flying secret information to Paris.

Normally, all Western spies are warned to *never* attempt to utilise the airlines for espionage purposes. Security control is so great over aircraft in Iron Curtain countries that using flights for conveying secret information is perilous. Every aircraft due to fly abroad is thoroughly searched by security agents before being towed out on to the tarmac; the air crews, passengers and airport personnel are all subject to frequent snap searches. But Wanda was able to overcome these difficulties very simply. She recruited a member of a regular air crew flying to the West, a stewardess. But this woman was not simply a stewardess, she was a trusted member of the Polish Communist Party and also in the employ of the Polish Secret Police. Her specific job was counter-espionage—to spy upon the other members of the crew and the passengers. The methods by which Wanda recruited such a valuable agent cannot be revealed, but by doing so, this French woman master spy provided herself with a first-class communications system. The stewardess picked up microfilms from the dead-drop assigned to her and carried them aboard the airliner concealed within an innocent-looking container, such as a lipstick, a powder compact or a hair brush. When the airliner landed in Paris, the stewardess was careful to avoid talking to any foreigners before she visited the toilet. The airport toilet was a crude but efficient dead-drop which was visited, as soon as she left it, by a French Secret Service agent who had been waiting for the stewardess' flight to land and then recover the deposited espionage material.

Wanda used this stewardess for many years. But eventually the stewardess was promoted and transferred to a more important job at LOT headquarters.

The French Secret Service was so impressed by Wanda's effi-cient use of an airline stewardess that the same method was sug-gested to their master spy in Czechoslovakia. He too succeeded in recruiting a member of a Czech air crew to become a carrier.

But the honour of being the first to produce this espionage gimmick must be awarded to Wanda, who still works for the French Secret Service in Poland, and who may be even now using other Polish air crew members in the same way.

22 Bertha

Bertha was recruited by the West German Intelligence Service in 1961 and is still actively working as a master spy in the Communist German People's Republic. Curiously, her long, successful service to West German espionage was within a hair's breadth of being brought to an abrupt end, even before she began to spy.

Bertha is an influential official in the East German Government and ideally placed to obtain information for the West. West German Intelligence had reason to believe she could be wooed over and set to work against her own country.

Recruiting an agent in the target area is always difficult. Indeed, it is never attempted until there is every reason to believe the approach will meet with success. Months elapsed while West German agents investigated and studied Bertha's private and public life and assessed the chances of securing her cooperation.

Finally, at the end of October 1961 the decision was made that she should be asked to spy for West Germany. However, the man who would be Bertha's controlling officer was due for holiday leave and he decided her recruitment must wait until he returned to his office. During these vital few days, Bertha's future as a Western spy hung in the balance. On November 6th, 1961, West German spy-catchers arrested Heinz Felfe. They had discovered he was a Soviet master spy employed in General Gehlen's Federal Intelligence Service at Munich-Pullach Headquarters. This timely arrest saved Bertha's career as a spy because if the unmasking of Heinz Felfe had taken place a few days later, he would have by then received information about the new Resident Network Operator's recruitment and passed it on to Moscow.

The discovery of Heinz Felfe's espionage web within the heart of General Gehlen's organisation disturbed West German Intelligence officers deeply. There was a long period of checking and counter-checking to ensure that Heinz Felfe was not the only Russian master spy in Munich. The recruitment of Bertha was shelved meanwhile and it was not until 1963 that again the decision to enroll her as a West German Resident Network Operator was considered.

Bertha is not a beautiful woman; some men would be so ungallant as to describe her as ugly. Nevertheless, she possesses great charm, a compelling personality, a warm heart and hot blood. She is a loyal, trusted, influential member of the Communist Party and many of her comrades have become her lovers. Her spy network, involving more than twenty agents, informers and go-betweens, includes many men who have completely fallen under the spell of her physical charm.

When Bertha was first recruited as a master spy she already occupied a position that enabled her to obtain a great deal of important information. She was irked by the cautious Secret Service policy that restrains master spies from obtaining information directly themselves. The West German files on Bertha contain a number of microdot messages in which she expresses her frustration at this security measure:

'You are hundreds of kilometres away. How can you judge what is safe? I am working here and I am quite capable of assessing what is safe. Every day I see documents which are of the greatest importance. I am the only person in a position to microfilm them. If you insist on your ruling, you are cutting yourselves off from one of your finest sources . . . me!'

Bertha enclosed with this communication proof that she had disobeyed orders—a microfilm of important documents that had crossed her desk. This action placed her superiors in a quandary. They needed the information that only Bertha was able to obtain, but they did not wish to endanger the espionage network she had carefully built up.

They decided upon a compromise and below is a copy of the microdot instructions they sent to Bertha:

'You are permitted to microfilm documents yourself only in exceptional circumstances, and only if the information is of vital importance. You must yourself be the judge. But remember that your spy network is more important than any single document. Take no risks.'

Bertha replied in her typical robust way :

'I am not crazy. It's my neck that's being risked.'

Bertha carried on her spying without a hitch until the autumn of 1968 when the Soviet Russian and East German Counter-Intelligence Service realised there was a continual leak of vital information to the West. A large-scale spy-catching operation was launched and every suspected person was placed under secret surveillance. Enthusiastic spy-catchers can imagine that any innocent action is suspicious and many people were arrested, interrogated and tortured. Bertha and a number of her agents and informers came under suspicion but, because of her influential position, Bertha received a hint that security officers were about to strike and issued a May-Day signal which sent all the members of her espionage network underground. Despite repeated interrogations, tricky questions and verbal traps that security officers prepared for unwary suspects, Bertha came through the screening classified as 'perfectly clean'. She had chosen her agents with such care that all of them too survived the screening.

Having launched this security check-up, the Russian and East German spy-catchers were under an obligation to produce results, so a number of innocent scapegoats were interrogated and tortured until they 'confessed' to being spies. The Secret Police proved they had done their job, their superiors were satisfied and the pressure on Bertha's espionage network eased. But now, having passed through a strict security screening, Bertha's position was greatly strengthened. When the dust settled she activated her espionage network again and shortly afterwards, to her delight, she was promoted and elected as one of the delegates to be sent to Moscow with an East German mission, for 'secret talks' with Soviet leaders. Within twenty-four hours of her return to East Germany she was transmitting to her West German Intelligence directors a full report of the secret talks, which involved the Soviet Union's military and political plans for Berlin, Europe, the Middle East, Africa and South America.

For seven years Bertha has proved that a woman master spy can do the job, by operating almost non-stop from within the very heart of Moscow's most favoured satellite country.

23   Shura

Although the philosophy of pure Communism recognises the equality of men irrespective of colour, race, creed or economic status, the Government of Israel has always felt uneasy about the anti-Semitic trends that Soviet Russia has adopted at different times. Stalin, the power-crazed dictator who influenced Russia so strongly and disastrously for so many years, at times suffered delusions; he imagined organised groups of revolutionaries were planning to overthrow him. Israel was alarmed because from time to time there were officially sponsored outbreaks of anti-Semitism in the Soviet Union, which resulted in the persecution of citizens simply because they were Jews.

When Moscow instructed the Communist President of Czechoslovakia to stage a public treason trial, in order to purge the Czechoslovak Communist Party of any members whose loyalty was in doubt, the long list of charges significantly accused the victims selected for purging as being Zionist conspirators. Subsequently, after lengthy negotiations between the Israeli Government and the Kremlin-controlled Czechoslovak Government, agreement was reached that a large number of Czech Jewish emigrants should be allowed to leave Czechoslovakia to take up residence in Israel. Nevertheless, at the moment of embarkation, these Jewish emigrants had their exit permits withdrawn by the Czechoslovak Government and were told they could not be permitted to travel to Israel.

In more recent years Moscow has declared its opposition to Israel in an even more active fashion. The Kremlin has openly supported the Arab states in their policy of aggression towards Israel, and has supplied President Nasser with war material, at the risk of incurring political and military problems on an international scale.

It is not surprising that Israel thinks it very necessary to keep well informed about Russia's political and military policy and has a number of master spies at work inside the Soviet Union.

The most successful Israeli master spy in the U.S.S.R. is a woman known by the code name of Shura, though Shura is *not* Jewish. She is a blue-eyed blonde of Russian stock who has never set foot outside the Soviet Union in her life.

Following Western policy, Israeli Intelligence officers selected Shura for an agent because she was already strongly entrenched in the target area. She occupies the post of a civil servant in one of the Soviet ministries. Israeli Intelligence officers kept this woman under observation for a long time before they felt confident enough to approach her and enrol her as a master spy. They chose their moment for recruiting carefully—when Shura was enjoying her annual holiday in a Soviet Black Sea resort. And Shura is still working for Israel today, a proven and very efficient master spy who has built up a network comprising twenty-seven agents and informers.

Shura has a good, natural 'cover' background. When she was still at school she was marked down as possessing the makings of a civil servant, but Shura has other advantages as well. The man with whom she has formed a close and intimate association is a K.G.B. officer; his position as a Soviet officer spreads a cloak of protection around her which makes suspicions about her loyalty even more unlikely.

Shura is tall, slim and attractive but not a very good mixer. She rarely goes to parties or the theatre unless accompanied by her K.G.B. lover. And since her lover's duties take him away from Moscow for long periods, Shura spends much of her spare time at home, reading and studying. Many of her superiors regard this as a good trend and respect her as a worthy citizen while they inwardly criticise her colleagues who seem bent only upon enjoying themselves at wild parties.

So Shura, having successfully established the reputation of being a semi-recluse, devotes herself to espionage without fear her precious time will be eroded away by friends clamouring to take her to a cinema or a football game.

Before Shura was recruited, Israel already had a spy network established in Moscow, so Shura was given the opportunity of taking this over if she wished to do so. But she was cautious. She turned down the offer. She knew too well the risks she was running and preferred to take her time and build up her own spy network comprised of agents and informers that she herself had recruited. She devised her own ingenious dead-drops and because of the ever-vigilant Soviet Secret Police she chose her go-betweens from the ranks of workers catering to the public: tram-conductors, railway ticket collectors, post office counter clerks, and shop assistants who meet hundreds of strangers daily in the normal course of their work. Such humble workers were ideal as go-betweens, having a small packet slipped to them by an unknown man or woman and passing it on to yet another unknown person when a codeword was spoken. The links between Shura's agents, go-betweens and informers are such that should any solitary link in her espionage network be grasped by the Russian Secret Police, the rest of the network cannot be traced.

Shura's dead-drops are ingenious and, although she scorns the traditional type of dead-drop used by spies, sometimes they are necessary. On one occasion the use of a traditional dead-drop almost rendered useless the important information Shura was relaying to Israel.

It happened when an agent came into possession of secret information which was so important that Israel had to receive it swiftly. Shura signalled the agent to deliver the microfilm to dead-drop 7, which was only used in an emergency. The dead-drop 7 was a cubicle in a public convenience. Shura went personally to collect the microfilm but to her dismay found the cubicle had been locked up by the toilet attendant who had decided to use this particular cubicle to store her brooms and cleaning utensils. Shura could not obtain the pass key, the lock was too strong to break and she was reluctant to bring suspicion upon herself by insisting being allowed to use this cubicle. She had to send another urgent signal to her agent requesting that a copy of the microfilm be left in another emergency dead-drop. All this wasted precious hours, but Israel eventually received the microfilm in good time.

It is always bad policy for a master spy to be in possession of microfilms. But the difficulties of spying in the Soviet Union are so great that this risk frequently has to be taken.

On one occasion, Shura was almost caught red-handed while in possession of an incriminating microfilm on which one of her agents had photographed the blueprints of a top-secret guided missile. During her lunch-hour break she collected it from a dead-drop and returned to the ministry offices with the microfilm snugly lodged under her breast within the secrecy of her brassière. She entered the ministry building, walked to the lift and stepped inside. The lift operator closed the door, stared out at the descending wall and commented casually :

'Looks like we'll have a busy afternoon. The Secret Police have dropped in for a snap search.'

Nobody can be trusted in the Soviet Union. Nobody can be sure a best friend won't curry favour with the régime by reporting carelessly phrased words to a K.G.B. officer. Shura knew that if she asked the lift attendant to return her to the ground floor, he might later remember he had warned her of the presence of Secret Police and grow suspicious. She instantly decided she would have to face up to a search; but she also knew a search could be disastrous. The gimlet-eyed Secret Service men do not merely turn out office desks, filing cabinets and cupboards; men employees are obliged to turn out the contents of their pockets and women have to surrender up their handbags and purses; furthermore, it is normal procedure for a number of men and women employees to be selected at random to be stripped and searched. Shura knew that if she was chosen for a strip-search she would face detection, interrogation, torture and death.

Precious seconds fleeted past as the lift ascended.

The microfilm was encased in a tiny aluminium container.

The lift operator's shoulders were towards Shura. She thrust her hand into her bodice, palmed the microfilm, brought her hand to her mouth and swallowed!

The microfilm container was small, but not that small! It passed down into her throat and lodged there.

Suddenly, Shura was choking. She wheezed and tears streamed from her eyes as she fought for breath. The lift operator turned and stared at her in astonishment. Her crimson face was already turning bluish and her hands grasped frantically at her throat. The lift operator had no inkling of his passenger's ailment but instinctively did the right thing. He spun Shura around and thumped her vigorously on the back. His remedy worked. Shura gave a long, gasping intake of breath and the ominous blueness left her cheeks.

'The sweet I was eating went down the wrong way,' she told the lift operator.

'My little girl did the same thing last week,' he told her. 'It scared me out of my wits.'

When Shura stepped out of the lift a security officer was waiting there. He checked Shura's name against the list of employees.

The security probe was thorough. The agents searched every nook and cranny of the offices. The employees were hoarded into a waiting room under the watchful eyes of two spy-catchers while the search was made. Then, as Shura had known was inevitable, six men and six women employees were selected at random and were taken away to be stripped.

Shura was not among them. She had suffered agonising asphyxiation in the lift, but she would have willingly undergone that experience again in preference to the awful tension of waiting to learn if she was to be stripped while in possession of incriminating evidence.

The next day Shura recovered the microfilm container and shortly afterwards it was on its way to her superiors in Israel.

Shura is still supplying her Israeli Secret Service chiefs with recordings of secret Kremlin conferences about Russian strategy in the Middle East, gives lists showing the quantities of armaments delivered to the Arab countries, the names and numbers of Russian technicians working for the Egyptian Government, and the Kremlin leaders' political attitude towards the increasing strength of Israel's economy.

Regrettably, the trend of political events seems to indicate that Israel will have great need of Shura's services for many years to come.

24 Vera

The construction of an elaborate espionage network, with dead-drops, go-betweens, coded advertisements in newspapers and all the devices employed by spies, has many times proved its value by saving the lives and liberties of agents and their master spy.

The Americans still have today an efficient espionage network in Prague which would not now be functioning if the precautions devised for the protection of spies had not been rigorously adopted.

In Prague, in 1966, police officers investigating a burglary developed suspicions against a man and swooped upon him. The police needed evidence and searched his premises, hoping to find stolen goods. As it happened, their suspicions were quite unjustified, but an alert police sergeant, while examining the suspect's writing desk, discovered a secret drawer. Inside this drawer was a microfilm camera! The police had searched for a thief and found a spy. The suspect and the microfilm camera evidence were handed over to the State Security Police.

The spy had only himself to blame for his misfortune. He had disobeyed orders. He should never have been found in possession of a microfilm camera. He had received strict instructions his camera was to be left in a dead-drop until required. His laziness, and his mistaken conviction that the secret drawer was safe, led to his interrogation and torture.

The spy did not break easily. At first he assumed an air of bewildered innocence, swore he had no knowledge of the secret drawer, suggested the camera must have been hidden in the writing desk when he bought it and passionately declared his faith in the Czechoslovak régime.

The microfilm camera was examined by specialists and the spy was confronted with blown-up photographs of his finger-prints found upon the camera. Proved to be a liar by this indisputable evidence that he had handled the camera, the spy could only stubbornly continue to deny the truth. He stuck to his story that he was not a spy and nor had he any knowledge of the camera.

The Secret Police officers had no doubt the man was lying. Experienced spy-catchers have many means at their disposal to persuade unwilling people to talk; from depriving prisoners of sleep, to applying severe electrical shocks to their genital organs. They had no doubt the man they were interrogating would finally tell all, and they were proved right.

A weak link had been discovered in a spy chain, and except for the careful construction of this American espionage network, all the other spies involved might well have been arrested at this point. The tortured man told all. But the information he knew was not enough to assist the spy-catchers. Their victim knew nobody else in his spy ring, and his only connection with it at all was through a dead-drop. Experts gave close attention to their unlucky prisoner until they were convinced they had squeezed every word of truth and knowledge from him. But they learned little of any value.

The State Security Police had kept their victim's arrest a secret, and they decided to make full use of what little information they had obtained from him. They knew now the location of the dead-drop, and at a meeting in the Ministry of State Security it was planned that a twenty-four-hour watch would be kept on the dead-drop until it was visited by the next spy-link in the espionage network.

However, one of the administrative heads of the Ministry for State Security, a woman whose cover name is Jirina, was a senior agent in the very American espionage network that the Secret Police officers planned to trap. And the master spy of this network also holds a high administrative position in the Czechoslovak Government and is known by the code name of Vera.

This was an emergency and justified Jirina's breaking all

security rules and conferring with Vera. And between them they devised a clever plot : the Secret Police officers were waiting for a victim to step into a trap at the dead-drop; very well, Vera and Jirina would provide them with a victim. But who? By a ruse they could have encouraged a completely innocent person to walk into the trap and brought the investigations of the Secret Police to a dead end. But Vera and Jirina improved on this idea and, at the same time, saved an innocent person from suffering.

For some time Vera had entertained strong suspicions about the loyalty of one of her agents who was known by the code name of Jan. Not only was the background to Jan's enrolment as a spy in doubt, but he behaved suspiciously. Furthermore, a good deal of the secret information he obtained and passed on was dangerously misleading. Vera had sound reason to believe this man was a counter-agent who was endeavouring to worm his way into her spy network. This was an ideal opportunity to put her suspicions to the test.

Vera flashed an urgent, secret signal to Jan, instructing him to collect a microfilm from the same dead-drop that was under observation by the Czechoslovak Secret Police. Jan walked into the trap and was arrested.

In her post at the Ministry of State Security, Jirina was able to learn what transpired later.

Like all good spies, Jan at first denied everything. Denials are a formality which could be dispensed with because a suspect always talks—finally. But it is a point of honour among spies that they must make a token refusal to talk, to prove their loyalty, so Jan received the 'treatment'. To Vera's relief, Jan confessed he was a Soviet spy who had been instructed by Moscow Secret Service headquarters to build up his own spy web within Czechoslovakia. Jan's passionate protestation that he was also trying to worm his way into another espionage network that supplied the United States with vital secrets was simply not believed by his interrogators. Thus, as a result of Jirina's and Vera's cool thinking, not only was their espionage network saved from destruction, but also, any suspicions about its existence was directed towards Moscow.

Vera is a good example of how the American policy of enrolling a master spy in the target area can pay dividends. The United States Secret Service agents decided early in the spring of 1964 that Vera was ideal spy material. She was contacted, recruited and given a crash course in espionage; by mid-summer she had established a compact network of agents that within a year grew to twenty-eight members. Since Vera has adopted other methods, it can now be revealed that for a long time, many of the magazines published by 'Orbis', in Prague, were sent overseas containing microfilms that regular subscribers received and passed on to Washington.

In Western countries master spies can make full use of classified personal advertisements in newspapers for giving coded instructions to their agents. But in Russia's satellite countries, including Czechoslovakia, the Press is so strictly controlled that even people inserting harmless classified adverts can come under suspicion. So Vera was obliged to use other methods to communicate with her agents and she did so with great ingenuity. Since she is still operating in Prague it is not possible to reveal details about these methods, for obvious reasons.

In the autumn of 1969, Vera's espionage network came close to disintegration; not because of the activity of the Czechoslovak State Security Police, but because of political events unconnected with espionage.

The new liberalising Czech Government, under the leadership of Dubcek, had defied Moscow's orders about political strategy and policy. The Kremlin leaders were angry and virtually occupied Czechoslovakia by force of arms. As the Red Army troops invaded Czechoslovak territory under the guise of conducting Warsaw Treaty military manœuvres, Russian Secret Police and Secret agents poured into Prague, assumed control of all the administrative offices and in effect became the government. Intent on destroying any resistance that might be offered to Moscow by loyal Czechs and Slovaks, an immediate purge of Czechoslovakia's entire bureaucracy was launched. High-ranking civil servants who had served in their posts for many years were abruptly ejected from the civil service merely on suspicion that they might not be in favour of Moscow's intervention in Czechoslovak affairs.

Vera, a handsome and highly intelligent brunette of thirty-nine, was so efficient and so adaptable that she moved with the political times. She came through the purge unscathed. Jirina, Vera's second-in-command, also survived the purge. This strengthened their position. The new administrative set-up was now completely trusted and Vera and Jirina were able to cover up effectively for many of their agents. Nevertheless, the purge was very thorough and of Vera's twenty-eight agents only eleven survived the ruthless screening by Russia's Secret Police and retained positions which gave them access to important military and political information. But those agents who were transferred to less important work were never suspected of having been members of a spy ring.

Vera was not discouraged by this big set-back. She set to work resolutely and by February of 1970 had recruited five new agents who are employed in the Skoda Works and other armament factories. Once again information and technical data began to flow steadily across the Atlantic.

The seventeenth member of the new spy ring recruited by Vera is a senior woman official in the Information Department of the Central Committee of the Czechoslovak Communist Party. This agent has direct access to all top-secret communications with the Kremlin. Through this agent, Vera has been able to keep the United States informed about Russia's political strategy in the Middle East, in Berlin, in the Vietnam War, and about the international Red Fifth Column which provokes strikes and riots in selected cities of the free world.

Vera has proved herself to be an invaluable woman master spy whose cover job in Prague is so sound that she is above all suspicion.

Could a man have inspired so much trust and confidence in those he is betraying as has this woman?

25   Lotus Blossom

Red China is growing rapidly and becoming a dominant power in world affairs, and the West does not under-estimate the importance of gaining full knowledge of Peking's military and political developments. But Western espionage within Red China is confronted with enormous difficulties. The West tends to regard conditions within the Soviet Union and her satellite countries as an alien way of life, but compared with China's philosophy and morality, both East and West are in harmony about man's needs. Mao Tse-tung's culture is so divorced from Western ideas of civilisation and Red China is so drastically zealous in pursuit of fanatical ideals, that it has almost no common ground for understanding with either the Soviet Union or the Western world.

Mao Tse-tung's Revolution has inspired two generations of Chinese people with ideas so revolutionary and sweeping in their application that Western minds find it hard to believe these revolutionary ideas are actually accepted and believed. But young Red Chinese fanatics really do believe in the sanctity of Mao Tse-tung as a Chinese saviour, and hold to the belief so passionately they are even willing to denounce their parents, relatives and closest friends as traitors if they think it is in the interest of the Chinese State to do so. Red Chinese society is permeated by thousands of Chinese Secret Police who spy upon everyone. But the public regards this as being highly desirable rather than as a threat to individual liberty. The arrest, torture and execution of a suspected person against whom no proof of any guilt is produced is regarded as a very necessary security measure and essential for the welfare of the State. The West would regard this as a shocking violation of the rights of man.

In a country where everyone who does not agree implicitly with Mao Tse-tung is regarded as a traitor, the gathering of information by spies is not only perilous but is impeded by economic and social restrictions that render espionage almost impossible. Nevertheless, the West has to know what is going on in Red China and despite the difficulties, political, economic and military, information does filter through to the West.

Lotus Blossom was the code name of a Western agent and it is to the great credit of the British Secret Service that they ever succeeded in enrolling this Red Chinese woman as their master spy. I cannot give any details about how the West succeeded in recruiting such a trustworthy master spy in the target area, but there is no doubt Lotus Blossom was an excellent choice. She was one of the many fanatical young women followers of Mao Tse-tung. She brandished his 'Little Red Book' at meetings, had memorised every word of it and had dedicated herself to spreading the 'Teachings of the Great and Beloved Leader of the Chinese'. Despite her youth and beauty, her delicate skin and porcelain fragility, she dressed in the dull, grey jacket and trousers of Mao Tse-tung's army and trained to fight the 'Wicked Western Capitalists'. She was a trusted Communist and held an important job in Peking's hierarchy.

Lotus Blossom was recruited to the West by a British Intelligence director, though she had never set foot outside Red China. She was given a short intensive training in espionage and thereafter she worked devoutly for the Free World.

Building up a spy web was a difficult and dangerous task for the new master spy, and six months after starting her new career, Lotus Blossom had recruited only two agents. But Britain's Intelligence directors did not harry her; they sympathised with her difficulties—it was better that she built up her espionage network slowly but confidently. Whitehall knew the enormous difficulties with which she had to contend. The usual tools of the professional spy, the microphones, microfilm cameras and transmitters, were not only difficult to smuggle into Red China, but most arduous to conceal once they reached their destination. The Chinese housing problem is acute and most Chinese families live in communal rooms under a semi-military régime. Every Chinese is on his or her honour to watch everyone else, and to report any suspicious activity to any of the many thousands of Communist Party members or Secret Police. Social privacy is almost non-existent. The ritual turning-over of citizens' simple possessions by the numerous Communist 'snoopers' deprives all individuals of privacy and the concealment of espionage equipment is virtually impossible.

Nevertheless, Lotus Blossom received and managed to conceal the espionage equipment supplied to her by her British Intelligence directors. She dared to use it and sent to London all information she obtained through the two trusted agents she had appointed.

As time passed, Lotus Blossom became more confident and experienced. She recruited additional agents—not only in Peking but also in Shanghai and other Red Chinese centres—and soon her spy web numbered eight agents and informers.

By Western standards, this was a humble espionage network, but in Red China it was miraculous Lotus Blossom had entrenched herself so deeply. Her small outpost of espionage yielded results far in excess of Britain's hopes. This was due to the fact that Lotus Blossom had chosen all her agents most carefully after long consideration and that they proved most reliable. Through them, she was able to supply London with up-to-date information about Red China's atom bomb progress, with inside information about Sino-Soviet relations, and also about Mao Tse-tung's espionage rings in the West. Whitehall received advance information about Mao Tse-tung's plans for Hong Kong, Vietnam and Cambodia, as well as about the Chinese dictator's ambition to challenge the Kremlin and become the leader of the World Communist Movement.

Like Vera in Prague, Lotus Blossom and her espionage network almost came to grief because of a political purge. Despite the ceaseless search for people who are not true believers in the Mao Tse-tung faith, Red China periodically conducts a greater and intensified witch-hunt to smell out the opponents of the régime, the disbelievers, and even those who are not enthusiastic enough towards the Peking régime.

Lotus Blossom at first seemed to be above suspicion. The influential leaders of Mao Tse-tung's movement knew she was fanatically loyal. Nevertheless, she was watched and interrogated and for several weeks suffered nervous tension, not knowing if by some unguarded gesture or word she had betrayed herself. But to her relief, she was finally passed out as 'thoroughly trustworthy'.

But one of the agents she had first recruited was not so lucky. He, too, was a young fanatical supporter of Mao Tse-tung's policy, but he had incautiously expressed a slightly off-beat attitude towards one of Peking's rulings. He was investigated, interrogated and judged to be a 'renegade in the employ of Moscow'.

There were many such cases, and like the victims of the Inquisition, they were obliged to march through the streets as penance for their crime of heresy, and expose their persons to the rage of the populace. Bruised, battered and bloody, the 'renegades' reached the end of their 'parade of shame', only to be interrogated once again.

Lotus Blossom's agent was interrogated so 'enthusiastically' that he did not survive, and his mutilated body was carried off to the burial pit.

The agent's death undoubtedly saved him from the extremes of torture because one more belated search, after his death, resulted in the discovery of his microfilm camera. Had this incriminating evidence been discovered before he was murdered, his death would have been lingering and terrible.

The discovery of this microfilm camera was a bombshell to the Secret Police. It proved an Imperialist espionage network was actually operating in Shanghai. Mao Tse-tung ordered: 'It must be uprooted!' As a result one of the greatest investigating probes was launched that the harbour city has ever known. And it *still* goes on. Hundreds of innocent people have been arrested and subjected to inhuman tortures while the enthusiastic and fanatical public applauds each new arrest, interrogation and torture. Snap searches are planned and scores of secret agents descend upon an area and comb it thoroughly. Not even a needle in a haystack can escape detection by such a horde of spy-catchers.

In October of 1969, Lotus Blossom escaped detection by minutes. She believed herself to be in a safe hideout and had just finished transmitting an important message when she learned the location where she was was to be cordoned off, and that scores of spy-catchers were combing the district. The area was a collection of ramshackle huts that could easily be taken apart by determined men.

Lotus Blossom knew instantly she had no hope of concealing her short-wave radio transmitter from the sharp eyes of the searchers—she was aware that her only hope of survival was to get rid of the treacherous espionage evidence. But the speed with which the spy-catchers descended upon the district placed her in danger of being caught red-handed while doing it. She had only one recourse. With a stab of remorse—because so much risk was involved in smuggling a radio transmitter through to her—she raced to the roof of the building, sparked off the self-destruction mechanism the apparatus contained and hurled it as far as she could into a neighbouring garden. Seconds later there was a great, satisfying explosion as the transmitter blew to smithereens. At once, like a horde of hornets, the spy-catchers descended upon this pin-pointed area, swamped through the ramshackle buildings and rounded up all the inhabitants, Lotus Blossom among them. The explosion was investigated but the destruction device was so effective that none of the fragments gathered up by the spy-catchers hinted at the existence of a clandestine radio transmitter.

In July 1969, Lotus Blossom's spy ring comprised nineteen agents and informers. Every link in the network was sound and strong, which proved to be invaluable to the British Secret Ser-

F

vice because soon they were to lose their master spy.

Lotus Blossom, by virtue of her position in the Chinese Communist Party, was delegated to attend a conference, which entailed her leaving Peking. All the delegates were housed in a street of ramshackle wooden houses and during the night, while Lotus Blossom slept, there was an outbreak of fire. The flames swiftly spread from house to house as though a match had been applied to tinder soaked in gasoline. The first that Lotus Blossom knew of it was the smoke curling in under her door and the intense heat. Together with others who occupied her room, Lotus Blossom escaped death in the flames by jumping from the window. She was taken to hospital and treated for her injuries but she was so badly burned she died four days later.

Lotus Blossom's life was short and ended in stark tragedy. But for the short time she was employed by the British Secret Service she gave loyal service and supplied London with invaluable information. But even more important, she had built up an espionage network so efficiently that it did not disintegrate when she died.

Today, Lotus Blossom's spy web still continues to supply the British Secret Service with information, as though to prove that Lotus Blossom's dedication to the ideals of the West did not die with her.

26   A Brief Glance at Other Women Spies

Jana is a master spy who was recruited by the United States in Poland in 1967. She is a Trade Union official, travels widely all over Poland and is often delegated to visit other Iron Curtain countries to attend Trade Union Congresses. Her work brings her in close contact with many powerful politicians and, because she sometimes obtains information from them that she considers important, she made, in the early days of her service as a master spy, the grave mistake of making personal contacts with other members of her spy ring 'to save time'.

When Washington discovered this, Jana was sternly reprimanded. But like Bertha, the West German spy,[1] Jana was frustrated and complained she was 'wasting valuable time and opportunities'. But Washington was unrelenting. She was ordered to cut out from her spy ring all those links with which she had made personal contact and never use them again.

Jana obeyed grudgingly but within two years Washington's foresight was proved to be justified.

One of Jana's agents was a typist in a Gdynia shipping office. She came under suspicion, was arrested and a diligent search turned up her microfilm camera and a bugging device. The typist was subjected to the normal ritual of interrogation and torture and duly confessed to being a spy, betrayed her system of coded communications and indicated the whereabouts of her dead-drop.

Russian and Polish Security officers staked out the dead-drop, ready for any unwary spy who might walk into the trap. None did. Jana had been warned by another agent that the typist had been arrested and her May-Day signals to all her agents prevented

[1] See pages 144–7.

any member of her network approaching the dead-drop.

There is little doubt that if Washington had not insisted that Jana should cut out from her spy network all those with whom she had made personal contact, she might well have been arrested herself together with most of her agents.

The British Secret Service has a woman master spy in Moscow who has been given the code name of Yevgeniya. Yevgeniya herself is a member of the Communist Party, but she is only a medium-grade official in Intourist, the Russian travel agency.

A British Intelligence officer recruited Yevgeniya in 1963 and since then she has built up an espionage network of twenty-three agents and informers. She has followed the strict rule of never making personal contact with any of her agents or informers; with one exception and this exception was agreed to by the British Secret Service.

Yevgeniya's most important dead-drop is not only a place, it is also a person. Every woman visits a hairdressing salon and to do so frequently is not a suspicious event, even in Soviet Russia. When any of Yevgeniya's agents visits the hairdressing salon, the hairdresser removes from their curls the concealed microfilm and later, when visited by Yevgeniya, dresses into her hair these miniature containers.

Yevgeniya's espionage network is extensive. Her job at Intourist enables her to meet Russians travelling from all parts in Russia, and among them are many members of her spy ring. But Yevgeniya never permits any of them to make personal contact with her; whatever microfilm information they have in their possession they must take to their appointed dead-drop, never realising that the woman they may have just spoken to will be the ultimate recipient of it.

Indeed, when at work in the Intourist office Yevgeniya is especially careful to keep herself above suspicion. When it is necessary to deal with a tourist from abroad, she always calls in a colleague to assist her, so that at no time can it be said she has spoken privately with a foreigner. She is also extremely loyal to the Russian State and any hint of criticism dropped in her presence by a foreigner is immediately rebutted by her with a 'Party line' response. Her colleagues secretly believe Yevgeniya is too fanatical, and talks only with the voice of *Pravda*.

Two excellent sources of information for Yevgeniya are her sister, who is engaged in secret research work at Dubna, and her brother, who is a K.G.B. major. Family ties are strong and brothers and sisters, who are all loyal members of the Communist Party, can talk frankly about political, military and industrial trends, during which secrets are confidently aired, with the conviction they will not be repeated elsewhere.

The British Secret Service has received a great deal of valuable information from Yevgeniya's brother and sister without their being aware of it.

After the Hungarian uprising in 1956 the West German Secret Service made contact with a woman they gave the code name of Ilona. They recruited her as an agent and gave her a brief concentrated training in espionage. But as Ilona was about to begin her career as a master spy, she was summoned to an interview by the Hungarian Communist Party. She was told she had been under observation and it was believed she possessed the qualifications for being trained as a full-time executive member of the Hungarian Communist Party.

Ilona was relieved to learn there was no suspicion about her contact with the West German Secret Service, and she was delighted she was trusted enough to be made a paid official of the Hungarian Communist Party. But, as a result of the interview, her contact with the West was abruptly terminated. She was sent to Moscow for special training at the Lenin School.

For two years Ilona was brainwashed and conditioned to become a Communist Party executive member. On completion of her training she'd hoped to be sent back to her native country, but Moscow had other plans for her. She next served a three-year stint in the Hungarian Department of the Russian State Publishing House; thus, a total of five years elapsed before Moscow gave her orders to return to Budapest—in 1961.

The West German Secret Service had long ago abandoned their plan to use Ilona as a spy but, from interest, had kept a check upon her and knew how she had been engaged in Moscow. To their surprise, as soon as she returned to Budapest, she at once made contact with the West German Secret Service and again expressed her willingness to work for them. The offer looked suspicious. For five long years Ilona had lived in Moscow and breathed the conditioned fanatical air of Communism. It was probable that she had long ago confessed to her contacts with the West German Secret Service and was now about to be used by the Russians as a double agent.

West Germany accepted Ilona's service and put her to work, but the German Intelligence directors were cautious and at no time could Ilona have betrayed any other Western spy, or receive any information that could be of value to Moscow.

After two years on probation, during which time Ilona built up her own efficient espionage network, it was realised she was thoroughly trustworthy. She was *not* a double agent working for the Russians.

Ilona had been brainwashed and conditioned in Russian political philosophy for five years, yet she had not succumbed to this prolonged barrage of mental propaganda.

An efficient woman master spy, recruited by an Israeli Secret Service agent, operated in Prague under the code name of Marena. She was not Jewish but of Czech peasant stock; her father was a trusted member of the Czech Communist Party.

Marena was unusually intelligent and despite her limited education managed to obtain a job in Prague in the Czechoslovak Broadcasting House. There she discovered she had a great love of music and made full use of her employment to make friends of musicians and composers.

Like all master spies working behind the Iron Curtain, Marena had to build up a complicated system of dead-drops. She realised it was advantageous to use her friendship with the musicians who regularly played for Radio Prague and devised a complicated code which was approved by her superiors in Israel. When it was necessary for Israel to receive vital information as swiftly as possible, Marena prevailed upon her musician friends to play, as an addition to their scheduled programme, an extra piece of music which she declared she particularly wanted to hear; this was the ingeniously thought-out code and in this way Israel often obtained vital and urgent information direct from Radio Prague!

Marena no longer works for Israel.

When Russian troops occupied Czechoslovakia in August 1968, Marena was on duty at Prague Broadcasting House. She was one of the many employees besieged there by Russian soldiers until the doors were broken down. Later, all were subjected to intensive interrogation. Most of the Radio Prague staff were sent away to work in the Czechoslovak frontier region as a safety precaution and Marena's spy network broke down.

The French Secret Service recruited an extremely attractive and seductive Rumanian girl as a master spy in 1965 and gave her the code name of Yvette. She was employed by the Rumanian Government as a statistician. Her job involved travelling all over Rumania to various government factories and departments and, being young, vivacious and willing, she delighted in the friendship of a large circle of male acquaintances. She was cool-headed and efficient and built up an extensive spy ring comprising twenty-six agents and informers. But she infuriated her French superiors.

In official circles behind the Iron Curtain there is a great deal of fraternising among the top brass of all those countries. Yvette gained a certain reputation for herself as eager to give a man a wonderful time, and found herself invited to many official receptions, doubtless with the intention that the visiting top-brass should find enchanting and entertaining company available. Yvette basked in the popularity she enjoyed and could not resist feeling she was a reincarnated Mata Hari.

Whenever Yvette was to meet influential, foreign politicians she concealed on her person a miniature hair-wire recorder and then daringly encouraged her escort to discuss matters of State Security. The French Secret Service were at their wits' end to convince their master spy that, valuable though the information might be, the means of obtaining it did not justify the risk. But Yvette was headstrong and for five years the French Secret Service periodically received hair-wire recordings of conversations between Yvette and lovers in the privacy of her bedroom. These were not only interesting as far as information of military importance but they also served as a lesson on how to seduce a visiting official.

The French Secret Service many times seriously considered suspending Yvette and allowing her espionage network to disintegrate. But this would have been cutting off their nose to spite their face.

Yvette finally solved the problem for them by once again acting unpredictably. She was appointed a member of a Rumanian Trade Delegation visiting the West—and having travelled to London and New York she decided she preferred the West to the East and promptly defected to the West, declaring herself a political refugee.

The French Secret Service were angry she deserted her post as master spy in Bucharest, but Yvette was sincerely contrite, gave her superiors every assistance and within a few weeks another French master spy was at work in Bucharest, using the same spy network that Yvette had built up.

In 1962 the West Germans recruited as a master spy a Czechoslovak middle-aged woman secretary who worked in the Foreign Ministry, and who was given the code name of Jarmila. This quiet, unassuming woman began active field work in 1962 after having received a crash course of espionage training. She slowly but thoroughly built up a spy web that numbered fourteen members. Jarmila was obedient to her superiors' orders and never at any time contacted any other member of her spy ring; nor did she attempt to spy actively within the Foreign Ministry where she worked.

Between 1968 and 1970, the invasion by the Russians of Czechoslovakia, and the installing of Russian Security agents in all the Czechoslovak administrative offices, resulted in an extensive purge of all employees. Jarmila survived this drastic screening of the Czechoslovak civil service but four of her sub-agents were not so lucky. They were declared 'doubtful', were expelled from the Communist Party and sent to labour in the frontier regions of Czechoslovakia. However, as these words are being written, Jarmila has communicated to the West German Secret Service that she has already replaced two of the agents she lost and is working upon two more prospective agents.

The woman master spy that Britain employs in East Germany goes under the code name of Else. She was recruited in 1968— only a month after the Russian occupation of Czechoslovakia.

Else is a dress designer, comes from a respectable middle-class family and is regarded as a well-brought-up German fräulein, but a modern German fräulein whose ideals have marched with the times. She is a member of the East German Communist Party and considered so loyal to the party that she is frequently sent to Moscow as a delegate.

By February 1969 Else had constructed an espionage network of seventeen sub-agents and informers. And her spy web is still operating for the British as this book goes to press.

The Japanese Secret Service has successfully penetrated the security screens of Red China. They have a woman agent working for them who is employed at the heart of Red China's administration; and it can be revealed that she is on intimate friendly terms with Mao Tse-tung and his wife.

This woman master spy's code is Chia. She was recruited by Japanese Intelligence agents in 1964 and began operating that same year. Within two months she had appointed three agents and began supplying Tokyo with information.

At the beginning of 1970 Chia's spy ring comprised thirty-two agents and informers. On two occasions Chia's agents have come close to detection when Chinese Counter-Intelligence experts discovered Japanese bugging devices installed in rooms where secret conferences had been held. But despite intensive screening of personnel Chia and her agents escaped detection.

Chia and her well-functioning espionage network are still operating today.

Why is it that the Western method of recruiting a spy in the target area is so successful whereas Russians are not as much in favour of using this method?

There is only one conclusion to be drawn : despite all the efforts of the Secret Service experts behind the Iron Curtain to ensure that they have the loyalty of their people, by the use of concentrated propaganda, brainwashing and conditioning, there are quite a few obstinate individuals who still think for themselves, analyse history and events, and make their own judgments.

Those who decide to spy for the Free Western World from privileged positions within the Communist Party have not been swayed by monetary bribes. They are thinking people who have begun to believe that all is not right within their own social, economic and political orbit.

27 Western Women Spies, Spying on the West

War and politics are a filthy business. The two are closely bound up with each other because war cannot be efficiently waged without political conspiracy, and in quite a few countries politicians have no power without the backing of the armed forces.

Despite this, in some countries politicians are *not* men of power. They are the pawns of military strategy, who strut and bask in the public eye, as suits their egocentric natures, but who are, in fact, nothing more than puppets on a string to be used for propaganda purposes. The true men of power are those behind the scenes who control the armed forces and those who hold the reins of industrial and economic control. It is these men who make the decisions which the political puppets embrace and propagate.

Since war and politics is a corrupt business it is not surprising that its beastliness is pursued to the extremes. Thus espionage flourishes while every decent instinct in man is revolted by the thought of betraying people who have become friends, and by all the underhand methods that spying involves—from blackmail through extortion, to torture and quite often even to murder. Yet such is the twisted moral attitude fostered by the militarists and some politicians that the spy profession is frequently acclaimed as being honourable and praiseworthy.

No one can deny spies are very brave, nor that they are intelligent and able. But the task they voluntarily undertake is a disgusting one. No matter how it is dressed up with words such as 'patriotism', 'romance' or 'courage' to make it look respectable, the profession of spy rejects honesty, humanity and brotherly love.

Governments are so depraved that espionage is regarded as being not only necessary, but desirable. And since all governments are equally corrupt in this respect, there has even developed a kind of 'honour among thieves' policy between them.

It is known and expected that some of the consular and embassy staff will do all they can to ferret out the secrets of their host nation while they are enjoying diplomatic immunity. Even minor spying ventures are overlooked—much as a public house proprietor expects his counter staff to swindle him, and regards petty thieving as part of his overheads—unless the abuse exceeds reasonable limits. It is only when diplomats overstep the boundary of prudence and devote more of their time to espionage than to diplomacy that the host government requests that the diplomat be returned to his own country as a persona non grata. In due course the diplomat will be replaced by another who, for a time, will behave diplomatically.

With spying rampant and governments devoting fortunes to the ferreting out of other countries' secrets, and with the resources of their Treasuries readily available to espionage operators without too much scrutiny by accountants, the tendency is for espionage to spread itself and grow fat. The West spies on the East and the East on the West. Every country wants to know what's happening in the Middle East, in Africa, China, South America and everywhere else. With so much spying going on it is not surprising to learn that Russia spies on its own satellite countries, and in their turn those satellite countries that are less rigidly controlled by the Kremlin do their best to find out what is happening in the Soviet Union.

It is part of the dirty pattern of war, politics and espionage that the countries of the West also spy on each other. There seems no end to the espionage networks that penetrate and flourish in every country of the world.

One of the United States' women spies who spied on Britain had the code name of Patricia. She was recruited by Washington's

Intelligence agents in 1963 and operated very successfully in London.

Patricia was a mature woman of forty years old, blonde, business-like and self-assured. She was a spy in the target area who was approached and enrolled by methods known best to the Americans. She had a good cover. She was the manageress of a dry-cleaning establishment in London's West End, and was thus well placed in the heart of Britain's metropolis and within a stone's throw of Whitehall where all important political and military decisions are made.

In comparison with her colleagues who were sent to work behind the Iron Curtain, Patricia had an easy task. The liberty and freedom of the individual is respected more in Britain than in most countries of the world; a spy in London has to behave very erratically indeed to draw attention to herself.

Patricia was able to dispense with dead-drops. When two people meet in a pub for a drink, in a café over a pot of tea or in a restaurant for lunch, it is not considered as a suspicious act in Britain as it is in the East. Patricia could meet her agents, go-betweens and informers quite openly and without fear of jeopardising the safety of the spy ring she had set up.

Washington was anxious to have specific information and Patricia was charged with devoting all her energies to this end. She was efficient and over a period of many months her network of informers and agents ferreted out every detail of the specific subject that interested U.S. Intelligence Headquarters. She passed the information on to the American Secret Service without ever coming under suspicion.

The British Secret Service is equally capable of treachery towards their friends across the Atlantic. They too recruited a woman master spy in the target area and confidential files give her cover name as Gene with full details of the results achieved by her.

Britain's Intelligence directors marked Gene down as a possible recruit when it was learned she was to be posted to London from Washington. When she arrived in England she was delighted to find a warm welcome awaiting her; a round of parties, invitations to dinners and concerts, and many new and interesting friends. There was one young man she became extremely fond of and, as though sensing this, his competitors melted away. Gene didn't mind. She was very happy to spend all her evenings with the young man who was, of course, a British Secret Service agent. Even before Gene's duty tour in London had ended, she was supplying him with classified information from Washington's files, and when she eventually returned to the States she had already undergone a course of espionage training and was rated a fully qualified master spy.

In Washington, Gene followed the usual procedure and established a spy web of agents and informers and, over a period of years, supplied London with much secret information about the United States. What particularly interested Gene's superiors in Whitehall was not what was entered in official inter-governmental and inter-military communications but what was omitted from those communications, and also the behind-the-scenes reasons for these omissions.

France spies on the British and the Americans and is particularly interested in her neighbour, the Federal Republic of West Germany.

One very successful spy the French planted in Berlin in 1960 is still continuing her espionage activities today, and is identified under the code name of Frieda. She is a public relations officer, and in her job it is natural for her to come in contact with a great variety of people holding influential government posts in West Germany.

Frieda's sources of information provide her with a great many pieces of diplomatic information which proved invaluable to Paris during the diplomatic manœuvring with West Germany. And as the French made their weight felt in the Common Market negotiations, they knew quite well to what extent the West German Government had been secretly negotiating for better relationships with the Kremlin.

In turn, the West German Government is quite well aware it has spies in its midst who work not only for the East, but on behalf of the Allied Governments too. West German Counter-Intelligence does its best to discover, deport or imprison these spies, but this is merely a formality.

In a more active recognition of espionage the West German Government employs its own army of spies throughout the world. One of its woman spies, known as Lola, provides proof that West Germany's spies are as efficient as any employed by other countries.

Lola had a Swiss father and an Austrian mother. She was a Tourist Guide and Sports Instructor in Switzerland, which brought her into contact with a great number of influential men and women visiting this neutral country for the summer and winter sports. She set up small spy rings in Zürich and in Vienna, and her agents and informers collected valuable information from the secret conferences of industrialists and bankers in Berne. They also plundered politicians and delegates visiting Switzerland and Austria to attend international conferences for inside information about their governments' political and strategic policy.

This master spy's cover profession of Tourist Courier and Sports Instructor enabled her to travel widely throughout Switzerland and Austria without suspicion ever being aroused by her constant travelling.

Israel is a small country but it has one of the finest and most efficient of Intelligence Services. President Nasser became well aware of this to his great dismay, consternation and ignominy. The Egyptians' plan for a surprise attack upon Israel was known well in advance by the Israeli Government, and President Nasser's dream of a successful military offensive resulted in the débâcle of the Six Day War. Within a few hours of the Arab forces going into action, the well-informed Israelis hit back with lightning and stunning accuracy, demolishing the entire Egyptian Air Force. Later, the world laughed when an expensive rocket-launching pad, which had been secretly smuggled into Egypt from the Soviet Union, was attacked by a small force of Israelis dropped from a helicopter, scooped up and flown back to Israel. This operation was not merely an act of daring bravado—it was a perfectly planned operation. Only accurate reporting by the Israeli Intelligence Service gave the operation any hope of success.

Israel has spies all over the world because the Jewish State is performing two tasks. Not only is it spying on all other countries, it is also seeking justice for the millions of Jewish victims of Nazi inhumanity. When Germany collapsed, many war criminals were brought to justice and punished for their crimes, but many powerful and very guilty war criminals used their influential positions to escape from Germany and take refuge in other countries under assumed names and identities. The Israeli Government is determined to keep faith with those who died in the Nazi concentration camps and has never ceased the search for these escaped war criminals. Eichmann, one of the most infamous of the Nazis, was found in South America and brought to Israel where he was obliged to stand trial before the Press of the world. But it was not easy to bring Eichmann to Israel and, no doubt, there are many other war criminals whom it has not been possible to bring before the court. In such cases, the efficient, tightly knit Israeli espionage service has not hesitated to impose its own punishment upon the criminal!

One of Israel's most valuable women master spies is listed under the code name of Ada. Egypt is Israel's biggest and most immediate enemy, and is therefore the country which occupies most of Israel's attention; therefore the work that Ada accomplishes in Egypt is of immense value to the Israeli Government.

Not too many facts can be given about Ada's activities because the Egyptian Counter-Intelligence is very alert and would quickly follow up any clues let drop about her true identity, but it can be disclosed that she occupies such an important position in the Egyptian administration that at present she is regarded as being totally above suspicion. At the many official functions President Nasser had to attend, he frequently had met her and greeted her as an old and trusted friend, yet it is the same woman who informed Israel when the Russian guided missile sites were to be installed, provided information about the Russians who were to take an active part in the Egyptian-Israeli battles and who provided Israel with President Nasser's complete plans for the invasion of Israel.

Italy is not an aggressive country and her neighbours do not feel a pressing need to man their borders for fear of an unexpected military offensive. Yet, possibly to keep in the swing with international governmental procedure, Italy employs a large army of spies who are working in almost every free country of the world.

One of Italy's most remarkable woman spies has the code name of Carlota. She is a woman of thirty-five, intelligent, with a very pleasing personality and holds an important administrative position in a big industrial plant in Stockholm. This is her cover profession for her more rewarding work as a master spy. Her network consists of twenty-two agents and informers.

That she is still a master spy for Italy after so many years is only because of the easy-going, tolerant attitude of the Italians.

For the first few years of her service, Rome was very satisfied with Carlota's work, praised her often and paid her well, but not well enough. Carlota is an expensive woman with expensive tastes and money swiftly melts away in her hands. Therefore, some years ago when a Soviet spy was astute enough to realise she was also a spy and made her an offer on behalf of his Moscow superiors, she accepted the proposition without hesitation and trebled her income without working appreciably harder. She continued to supply her Italian espionage directors with microfilms of blueprints, as well as with industrial and military secrets, but made duplicates which she also supplied to her Moscow employers.

Carlota worked as a double agent for some years before the fact was discovered in Rome. The Italian Secret Service had a master spy in Moscow who employed an agent inside Soviet Secret Service Headquarters. This agent learned that the information coming in from Stockholm was supplied by Carlota and informed his spy leader who, in turn, spilled the beans to Rome.

It is the practice of Intelligence officers to sever connections instantly with any spy they find acting as a double agent, because such an activity puts the spy's loyalty clearly in doubt and treachery in the future could have fateful results. But Carlota's Italian superiors also knew the information she supplied them so regularly was of great importance. They were loath to dispense with such an excellent source of information. So, with typical cheerful Latin tolerance, Carlota's superiors decided to allow her to continue acting as a double agent, after having reprimanded her severely. But a note was added to her file : under no circumstances in the future was she to be given any hint whatsoever in any coded messages of anything that might be of use to the Soviet Union.

Journalists and investigators are constantly revealing how widespread espionage has become and the man in the street, who once regarded espionage as being as improbable as James Bond's adventures, now knows he is quite likely to brush shoulders with professional spies as he goes about his everyday affairs.

It is a depressing thought. Spies are two-faced. They gain friendship and betray it for personal benefit. Still, it has long been said that 'women are forever deceivers'.

Is that delightful, charming woman we are likely to meet anywhere at any time really so sincere and honest? Or is there in some country, in some secret file, a code name under which she is listed as a master spy?

28 Spies are Hard to Catch

This book has made it clear that every year enormous sums of money are squandered by every country in the world on maintaining an army of spies who are equipped with every expensive modern aid to espionage. The information files amassed by every Secret Service department require enormous warehousing space for storage as well as hundreds of specialised and security-screened clerks to record, classify and correlate this information.

Doubtless, much of the intelligence data, which is obtained at great risk and despatched to Secret Service Headquarters by painfully devious methods, proves to be worthless when checked and cross-checked with other sources of information; much of it quickly becomes outdated. But every now and again a spy pulls off a big coup, which convinces Secret Service officers that their enormous administrative expenditure is justified.

Dr Klaus Fuchs is a striking example of how valuable just one spy can be in terms of money and research man-hours. The Americans spent untold millions of dollars on developing the atom bomb—Klaus Fuchs passed on vital information about it to the Russians and saved Moscow years of research time and billions of roubles.

Colonel Oleg Penkovsky, who was eventually unmasked and shot as a traitor to Russia, passed on to the West many valuable Russian secrets, and during the Cuban Crisis supplied the White House in Washington with diplomatic guidance which enabled President Kennedy to save the world from the very brink of war by preventing Castro from gaining possession of nuclear missiles.

Russian spies who obtained the secret details of the construction of the supersonic Concorde aircraft saved Russia a great deal of expense and hundreds of thousands of man-hours. By introducing a speedy assembly line the Russians succeeded in producing their own Konkordski supersonic aircraft for testing, before the French prototype was ready to take the air.

Whatever its cost in money and manpower, it seems that espionage has become an integral part of government and is likely to continue to be until the world is united as one great federated community. Spies will remain with us for many, many years. A few will be detected but the majority will continue about their nefarious business unknown except by their Secret Service chiefs.

Intelligence officers are not complacent about spies infiltrating their own country's administration. Whenever it is possible to lay bare an espionage network and smash it, they do so with alacrity. But they seldom have the opportunity. A spy may be a respectable businessman, a bus conductor, a governess, a workshop mechanic or a post office clerk. It is almost impossible to detect a spy unless the spy makes a mistake or is betrayed.

Behind the Iron Curtain, where an army of Secret Police agents are employed to spy on the mass of the people to ensure against political instability, the vigilance for possible spies is part and parcel of their routine job. It is known to the West that quite often Secret Police agents select an individual at random, and proceed to investigate his or her activities on the assumption the individual is a spy.

One woman master spy, working in Moscow on behalf of the West German Secret Service, has reported what happened when she was picked upon at random and subjected to investigation by the Russian Secret Police :

'Every time I return to my room, I check to see if it has been entered. Today, I discovered once again that an intruder had invaded my room, carefully searched all my drawers and cupboards and examined all my papers. I made my own routine search, expecting to locate a bugging device concealed somewhere. I did not find one. But what I *did* discover was a small metal capsule, the size of an aspirin, concealed under the collar of my overcoat. I was careful not to remove it and realised it must be a trailing signal.[1]

'The concealment of the trailing signal in my overcoat warned me that I was about to be subjected to more than the usual Secret Police routine investigation that we have grown so accustomed to here in Moscow. I did not know how strong were the suspicions against me. But it was important to protect my network and I took the calculated risk of flashing a coded signal which sent all my agents underground, and suspended all operations.

'From then onwards I proceeded about my business in the normal way, wearing my overcoat with its concealed metal capsule and making no attempt to ascertain if I was shadowed or not.

'This went on for two days and then I discovered that the trailing gadget had disappeared. How or when this was done I never discovered. But it did not seem reasonable that I should be cleared after only forty-eight hours of special vigilance. So I made a thorough search of all my clothing and belongings and found another trailing signal concealed in my briefcase.

'During the next few weeks I took care not to do anything that would arouse the slightest suspicion of my loyalty to the State, and during this time the trailing signal had its position changed half a dozen times. I once found it concealed within the foam-padding in one of my brassières.

'This security check continued for some six weeks during which time my nerves began to suffer from the strain. To have Secret Police agents watching me for so long seemed to indicate they had sound suspicions against me. I began to sleep fitfully, fearing the knock on the door in the middle of the night that would mean arrest by the Secret Police.

'Then after six weeks the trailing signal disappeared. Again I searched my clothing and belongings but this time, either it had been concealed too expertly for me to discover it or I was being

[1] A trailing signal is a miniature transmitter, sometimes no larger than a match head, which emits a continuous signal that can be picked up for a radius of five hundred yards. Anybody carrying a trailing signal would find it very difficult to throw off a shadower, who, with a miniature graduated receiver, would be able to pinpoint his prey among a crowd of a hundred thousand.

shadowed by police agents who had decided the use of a trailing signal not necessary in my case or . . . the Secret Police had cleared me.

'Another two weeks elapsed during which time I could discover no indication I was being tailed. I decided to risk another brief message to headquarters informing them I was suspending all operations for another three months.

'The three months elapsed and still without reason to believe I was still under suspicion, I again began operations and have continued to do so for the last three years without any hint that the Secret Police are paying me special attention.'

If enough Secret Police agents were to be employed to systematically check on all members of the public, it is obvious that at some time they are bound to detect a spy, an agent, an informer or a go-between. But in the West, spies are almost never caught by the use of a random selection of a suspect. Spies are usually unmasked either because of their own stupidity or betrayal by other spies.

Colonel Rudolf Ivanovich Abel was a Soviet Russian master spy who operated in New York for nine long years without bringing any suspicions against himself or his widespread espionage network. He would probably never have been detected had it not been for his betrayal by another spy. Colonel Hayhanen was another Soviet spy who defected to the Americans and surrendered to them all the information he had about Colonel Abel's espionage network in the United States.

A Swedish Air Force Colonel, Stig Wennerström, was a Soviet master spy who operated in Stockholm for fifteen years without drawing the slightest suspicion to himself. Stig Wennerström's long career in espionage was brought to an abrupt end by information supplied to the Swedish Secret Service by another Soviet spy who had sought refuge in the West.

When the Soviet master spy Klimov defected to the United States Secret Service in Helsinki, he betrayed other Soviet master spies: Heinz Felfe, Hans Clemens and Erwin Tiebel, three spies who had been operating in West Germany for ten years!

Gordon Lonsdale, yet another Soviet master spy, operated in London for six years and would probably never have been detected had it not been for the stupidity of one of his agents. The agent was Harry Houghton, an ex-Navy Master-at-Arms who had been consistently supplying Lonsdale with secret information from the Underwater Weapons Establishment at Portland.

Houghton was *not* a Russian-trained agent. He was recruited by Lonsdale and it seems that simple greed was the only reason that induced him to sell his country's secrets. And it was vanity and the desire to show off that brought about Houghton's downfall. He was a five-hundred-pounds-a-year clerk, yet villagers whom he warmly invited to his cottage could not fail to be impressed by the way it was increasingly and ever more luxuriously furnished. When he traded in his old, battered car and bought a shiny modern one, his neighbours' eyes widened in astonishment. How could a poorly paid office worker practise such extravagances? Talk in the village started the ball rolling. Discreet enquiries were instigated and the rest of the story is now history. Houghton eventually stood alongside Lonsdale in the dock at the Old Bailey and was pronounced guilty of spying against his country.

Sometimes the element of mere chance can bring about a spy's downfall.

In Switzerland, Security officers accidentally observed that an unlicensed short-wave radio transmitter was broadcasting messages at irregular times. The messages were intercepted and found to be in indicipherable code.

The Security officers set about locating the transmitter. This was not an easy task. If detector vans patrolled the streets the spy would see them and instantly cease his transmission. Remote detector devices had to be used and counter-intelligence agents eventually established that the transmitter was operating from within a block of houses. But in which house was the transmitter?

The Swiss counter-intelligence agents devised a clever method to pinpoint the house. During the transmissions each house in turn had its electric current switched off for a brief interval, and the transmission stopped during the instant the power supply was cut off in one particular house. The net was prepared and two

East-European spies were captured in the act of transmitting. A great deal of espionage equipment was also seized.

The news of this arrest was quickly flashed to spies all over the world by their Secret Service Headquarters and now it is only in an extreme urgency that a spy will transmit on an apparatus that works on the local electricity supply.

In the United States a Soviet spy was unmasked because of a chance accident.

A Highway Patrol car frequently received strange acoustical effects on its radio. The police officers at first thought little of this, but since this strange, shrill sound occurred frequently and was not received on other patrol car radios, its officers decided to have their broadcasting equipment checked.

The radio technician was intrigued. In his opinion the shrill whistling was a form of transmission. But who would want to transmit unintelligible sounds? Unless . . . high-frequency coded messages were being transmitted! The F.B.I. were consulted and the strange transmissions received by the patrol car were recorded. Code experts worked on the recording and reported that indeed high-speed frequency messages were being transmitted, but the code used was undecipherable.

The F.B.I. set out to locate the transmitter. It was observed that the patrol car intercepted these coded messages more strongly when it was on a main highway. F.B.I. agents followed the patrol car throughout its duty tours and maintained radio contact with it. After some days it was observed that a blue Chevrolet was usually parked somewhere along the highway when the patrol car intercepted the transmission; on the days when there were no transmissions, the blue Chevrolet was not to be seen.

The blue Chevrolet was eventually approached by F.B.I. agents and its occupant lost his nerve, pulled a gun and tried to shoot himself out of the trap. His car contained a powerful miniature spy transmitter which by rare chance was tuned to broadcast on the same wave-length as that received by the Highway Patrol car radio.

29 Women Spies who Trap Spies

Catching spies is not easy. But once there is reason to suspect someone is a spy, the methods of checking and proving the suspicions are well known and virtually a ritual in all Communist countries. The suspect is interrogated and then given the 'treatment'.

In the West, where a man's liberty is respected and guaranteed by law, the task of the spy-catcher is much more difficult. Therefore, when Western counter-intelligence officers have *only* suspicions that a person may be a spy, they frequently use their women agents as spy-catchers.

These women spy-catchers are selected especially for their attractiveness, their engaging personality, their intelligence and their willingness to make full use of their womanly charms. Stated bluntly, their job is to ingratiate themselves with the suspect, gain his complete confidence, obtain access to his home and belongings and inspire his trust. A woman can best do this by making herself fully available to a man in every way. And by this supreme treachery, which only a woman can practise with a suspected male spy, many Soviet and other Iron Curtain spies have been unmasked.

Ivan Skrypov was First Secretary at the Soviet Embassy in Canberra, Australia. He arrived to take up his post in Australia in June 1959, and enjoyed full diplomatic immunity which he used as a cloak while he set up an espionage network. He was not acting on his own initiative but was obeying orders received direct from Moscow Secret Service Headquarters.

Skrypov began operating the moment he arrived in Australia

and soon had a spy ring built up which began to relay information to Moscow about the experimental missile station in
Woomera.

The Australian counter-intelligence had reason to suspect
Skrypov was violating his diplomatic privilege, and enrolled a
woman spy-catcher whose specific job was to trap the man. She
contrived to meet him casually and, using the weapons only available to an attractive woman, she soon had the First Secretary of
the Soviet Embassy on a string, dangling her bait tantalisingly,
allowing him to nibble, drawing it away teasingly and finally
completely hooking him.

Soon, while exchanging confidences in moments of tender in-
timacy, she told him of the great sorrow of her life; the untimely
death of her lover caused by the neglect of the Australian administration, and of her interest in Soviet Russia. Skrypov was 'a man
of the world', a staunch Communist Party member who held
down an important diplomatic position; yet he fell hook, line and
sinker for the woman spy-catcher's story. He decided to recruit
her as one of his agents.

Meanwhile, every meeting he had with the woman spy-catcher
was secretly photographed by Australian counter-intelligence
agents and every conversation they held was taped by the woman
spy-catcher's miniature recorder. When the Australian counter-
intelligence deemed the time was ripe, they pounced on the espionage network and Skrypov was requested to leave Australia as
persona non grata. The evidence collected by the Australian counter-intelligence was duplicated and sent to Moscow so that
Skrypov's superiors should know to what extent their master spy
had made a fool of himself.

Yakov Lysvich was the Soviet Vice-Consul in New York. Previous to his arrival to take up his post, the American counter-
intelligence had become suspicious of another Soviet diplomat
named Semyonov. One of America's women spy-catchers was
mandated to trap Semyonov, and when Yakov Lysvich arrived
in New York, Semyonov was already deeply involved in a love
affair with the woman spy-catcher. It transpired that the philo-

sophy of 'all for one and one for all' appealed to the Soviet diplomats and very soon the Vice-Consul, as well as Semyonov, were both enjoying the feminine charms of the woman spy-catcher, who meanwhile convinced them she was completely enamoured of them both and of the Russian form of Communism. They let her in on many of their secrets.

In due course, photographic and tape-recorded evidence proved the espionage activities of both the Soviet diplomats. They were recalled to Moscow after their agents, informers and go-betweens were rounded up by the F.B.I.

Xavier Schmeisser had an excellent cover job in Switzerland which enabled him to supply Moscow Secret Service Headquarters with a great deal of important information about Swiss defence installations in relation to the N.A.T.O. Powers. But eventually he drew suspicion to himself by an unguarded action.

A woman spy-catcher was appointed to work on him. It took a long time but with patience, perseverance and womanly charm, the spy-catcher wormed her way into Schmeisser's espionage network and passed back information to the Swiss counter-intelligence that enabled them to round it up.

Georges Pacques was Deputy Head of N.A.T.O.'s Press Service, and worked in the N.A.T.O. building, only a quarter of a mile from the Arc de Triomphe in Paris. He was a Soviet spy.

Suspicion of Pacques was first aroused by the defection to the West of another Soviet spy, Goloniewski, who asked for political refuge and gave as much information as he could to the French Secret Service. Analysing this information, the French counter-intelligence suspected that Pacques must be involved in spying, but there was no specific proof of this. A woman spy-catcher was enlisted to obtain the evidence that would be needed to arrest Pacques and convict him.

The woman spy-catcher contrived to be introduced to Pacques, became his mistress, gained the run of his apartment and obtained access to all his private documents. Primed by the woman agent, the French counter-intelligence were able to pounce on Pacques in his luxury apartment at the very moment he was actually in possession of top-secret information for despatch to Moscow.

There are hundreds of documented records of women spies who have proved not only that they are equal to men in espionage duties, but that they are superior to men in the art of catching spies.

Moscow has not hesitated to make use of this great weapon of superiority that women can wield—the weapon of sexual attraction.

A West German tourist visiting Moscow was enraptured by an attractive Russian girl who declared herself passionately in love with him. He believed her . . . until he was arrested by the Russian Secret Police and evidence was produced that he was a spy courier.

An American reporter in Prague discovered that life in that grey city was much gayer when he shared his lodgings with a Czech girl he had met. She declared herself ready to leave her family and country and go with him to the United States when he was recalled. But his stay in Czechoslovakia was much longer than he had anticipated. It was spent in a Czechoslovak prison camp after evidence gathered by his Czech girlfriend was brought before the courts and proved him to be a member of a spy ring.

An old saying advises us to, 'Do right and fear no man. Don't write and fear no woman!'

As far as male spies are concerned there seems only one sound maxim that can stand them in good stead:

'Fear all women!'

Eve is efficient as a spy. But as a spy-catcher, she is deadly.

Index